Creative Activities and Ideas for Pupils with English as an Additional Language

Creative Activities
and **Ideas** for **Pupils**
with **English** as
an **Additional**
Language

Maggie Webster

Longman
is an imprint of

Harlow, England • London • New York • Boston • San Francisco • Toronto
Sydney • Tokyo • Singapore • Hong Kong • Seoul • Taipei • New Delhi
Cape Town • Madrid • Mexico City • Amsterdam • Munich • Paris • Milan

PEARSON EDUCATION LIMITED
Edinburgh Gate
Harlow CM20 2JE
United Kingdom
Tel: +44 (0)1279 623623
Fax: +44 (0)1279 431059
website: www.pearson.com/uk

First edition published in Great Britain in 2011

The right of Maggie Webster to be identified as author of this work has been asserted
by her in accordance with the Copyright, Designs and Patents Act 1988.

Pearson Education is not responsible for the content of third party internet sites.

ISBN: 978-1-4082-6777-6

British Library Cataloguing-in-Publication Data
A catalogue record for this book is available from the British Library

Library of Congress Cataloging-in-Publication Data
Webster, Maggie.
  Creative activities and ideas for pupils with English as an additional language/
Maggie Webster.
     p. cm
  Includes index.
  ISBN 978-1-4082-6777-6 (pbk.)
  1. English language--Study and teaching (Elementary)--Activity programs--Great Britain.
  2. English language--Study and teaching (Elementary)--Great Britain--Foreign speakers.
  3. Education, Elementary--Activity programs--Great Britain. 4. Creative activities and seat
work. I. Title.
  LB1576.W375 2011
  372.6'044--dc23
                                           2011023359

ARP impression 98

Set in 8.5/12 News Gothic BT by 30
Printed and bound in Great Britain by Ashford Colour Press Ltd

Tara TEW
Our little laughing Buddha

Alan
My enlightened one!

Contents

Chapter 4 – Activities and ideas for verbal communication 97

Chapter 5 – Activities and ideas for written communication 145

Chapter 6 – Activities and ideas for visual aids and interactive teaching 185

Appendices   243

Preface

Many trainee teachers ask me how to teach children who have English as an Additional Language (EAL) and my answer never seems to be what they are looking for. It tends to be quite long and complicated and so they seem to be disappointed that there isn't a 'quick fix' or simple solution.

Yet teaching EAL pupils does not have to be complicated and difficult, especially if you are aware of simple strategies that can be used in all areas of school life to support learning and teaching. It does, however, mean that you have to rethink how you differentiate and plan for individual needs. And so this book is designed to help you gain insight into some methods of teaching a pupil who has early stages of English.

Chapters 2 to 6 contain a selection of activities and ideas that can be used as time fillers, ways to develop socialisation and social interaction as an introduction to a variety of lessons or as a plenary. I would, however, recommend that you read Chapter 1 first as it explains the best approaches to teaching EAL pupils and encourages you to reflect on the pedagogy. Although the activities and ideas are mainly suitable for a primary school setting some are suited to and can be adapted for KS3. The advice in Chapter 1 is appropriate for any Key Stage.

Acknowledgements

Thank you to Ian Shirley (Senior Lecturer at Edge Hill University), who created the musical scores and suggested some great ideas and web links.

Thank you to Editors Catherine Yates and Katy Robinson, who have dedicated much of their time to make sure my ideas are presented brilliantly!

Publisher's acknowledgements

We are grateful to the following for permission to reproduce copyright material:

Figure 1 on p. 9 from Cummins, J., *Language, Power and Pedagogy* (Multilingual Matters Ltd, 2000); Figure 2 on p. 10 from Baker, C., *Foundations of Bilingual Education and Bilingualism*, 3 (Multilingual Matters Ltd, 2001), both courtesy of Channel View Publications/Multilingual Matters.

In some cases we have been unable to trace the owners of copyright material, and we would appreciate any information that would enable us to do so.

Chapter 1
How to teach pupils with English as an Additional Language

As a visitor to many schools, it always surprises me to see how they have altered over the past fifteen to twenty years. This has been due to the many changes in government legislation and, since the early 1990s, the inclusion of the internet and innovative technology. Teachers have had to re-evaluate their role and adapt their style of teaching to accommodate change, often without training or support. Yet, arguably, one of the most challenging changes has been the ethnographic make-up of a class of pupils.

The UK has always been a multi-cultural society that welcomes migrant workers. Indeed, London's Whitechapel was home to many French and Dutch silk weavers who contributed to the economy in the seventeenth century (Rule, 2008). However, it seems that in the twenty-first century immigration isn't solely the responsibility of inner cities. Since the UK became part of the European Union, there appears to be a more obvious increase in the various cultures and languages found in our rural communities and consequently in our schools.

Currently there are estimated to be over 7000 pupils who are recorded as having a mother tongue other than English in our schools (**www.teachernet. gov.uk**) and there are over 300 languages spoken in the homes of children who attend English schools (**www.multiverse.ac.uk**). Many schools in England have identified newly arrived pupils who speak little or no English and schools have turned to their local authorities for help, finding that there is little funding to support the growing need.

Although the previous Labour government identified £206.6 million of funding for an Ethnic Minority Achievement Grant, proving that bilingual education was high on the educational agenda, the Coalition government has been cutting public services and so such future funding is likely to be at risk. This means that teachers will again have to find their own way to support such pupils, often with little or no training in English as an Additional Language (EAL) pedagogy from the Initial Teacher Training Institutions in which they qualified (**www.naldic.org.uk**).

It is a fundamental right for a child to have an education and, as identified in the National Strategies, support for pupils who have English as an Additional Language (EAL) is an entitlement and not a need. We therefore need to know the best way to support a pupil who is newly arrived and has little or no English, as well as to understand how to develop the capabilities of those students who may have English as their second, third or fourth language and are almost fluent.

Who is identified as learning English as an Additional Language?

It is important to note that many textbooks about bilingual education use a variety of terms. These include:

E2L = English as a 2nd Language
ESL = English as a Second Language
ELL = English Language Learners
BEL = Bilingual Education Learners

Because many pupils can be fluent in more than one language, in the UK we tend to identify children as having English as an Additional Language (EAL).
EAL pupils can be categorised as:

- Pupils born in Britain who speak their home language(s) *and* English on entry to school
- Pupils born in Britain who speak their home language(s) but do not speak English on entry to school
- Pupils newly arrived in Britain speaking languages other than English
- Pupils in a class in which many others speak their home language(s)
- Pupils who do not share the language of the teacher
- Pupils in a class in which everyone else speaks only English

As a teacher it is important to know the variety of languages an EAL pupil can speak in addition to English so that you can evaluate his/her capabilities. Active use of two languages can have a positive impact on learning in general (Baker and Hornberger, 2001: 41) and so it may be useful to decipher how well the pupil speaks and writes their home language so that you can then decide how much English language input they may need, especially if their first language is one that has a different alphabet.

It is best to try not to assume that the pupil will have difficulty learning English purely because they are new to it. If he/she is competent in three other languages then this demonstrates clear awareness of how to learn a language and usually very good meta-cognition capabilities.

Stages of language acquisition

On average it takes a child five years to become fluent in a language, which amounts to a whole school career in either primary or secondary education. So if a child enters into your class in Year 5 do not expect them to be fluent native English speakers until they are in secondary school. It is an agreed understanding between educationalists such as Jim Cummins and Colin Baker that it takes two years to master basic language and between five and seven to become proficient in its more complex nuances.

An EAL pupil may improve their knowledge of the English language and be able to communicate what they need on a daily basis, possibly discussing TV shows, sport and things of interest, but it will take longer for them to be able to evaluate, analyse, criticise, persuade and describe with evidence, etc. I am not saying that an EAL pupil is unable to do these creative high-order thinking tasks. They innately have this capability in their home language, and, with practice in the new language and support from teachers, over time they should be able to do them in a UK classroom.

To assess an EAL pupil's level of language you need to measure them against a native English speaker of the same age. As a general rule, local authorities tend to break down the capabilities into four or six levels so that a teacher can assess where the child is at; however, Baker (2001: 169) refers to a threshold whereby children develop in three stages. When I was an EAL teacher in East London I used the following four stages as a guide.

Stage One (*usually a pupil who is newly arrived in the UK*)

The pupil uses survival language and phrases. They have little experience of the English language.

- Where is the toilet?
- Pass the pen/ball/cup/salt
- Please/thank you
- Can I have . . .
- Swear words
- What is that?

Stage Two

The pupil uses basic sentences that can be understood but may not always be grammatically correct. The vocabulary is extended and there is general communication about things of interest.

- Discussion about football, music, etc.
- Answering a simple question in class
- Some basic ability to justify their opinion about a mathematical or scientific finding
- Correct use of some technical vocabulary
- Ability to describe family and friends and events
- Can copy-writing and write basic sentences

Stage Three (*usually a pupil who has lived in the UK a while*)

The pupil is able to express some abstract thought and is able to express it

- Answering complex questions in class that require a justification or an explanation
- Writing a persuasive argument and taking part in a debate
- Understanding the task in the lesson without having to have it explained again by the teacher
- Describing something that they may not have had much (if any) experience of, such as a tube/train ride or the path of a river from its Source to its Mouth

Stage Four

The pupil is able to communicate as well as or even better than a native English speaker of the same biological age. They can converse in jokes and understand the cultural conventions of the UK. Being able to understand a joke can be quite difficult for a person learning a language because jokes are usually related to a shared culture. For example:

> Humpty Dumpty sat on a wall
> Humpty Dumpty had a great fall
> And his winter wasn't bad either!

To be able to understand this joke you need to know that 'fall' is an Americanism and has two meanings.

It is important to note, however, that a child who is not progressing through the stages in a suitable timeframe (e.g. a child who has been in the UK for five years and is still at stage 1 or 2) is likely to have an additional learning need. They may not have a good grasp of their home language and so this is having an impact on their understanding. They may also have a special learning need such as dyslexia and so a diagnostic test may be useful. This may need to be conducted in their home language.

How do you teach EAL pupils?

Immersion versus Bilingualism

There seem to be two schools of thought about how pupils learn a language: Immersion and Bilingualism. Jim Cummins is one of the most influential educationalists in this field and he states that pupils acquire fluency in English when they are totally immersed and exposed to it (Cummins, 2000: 34). However, others have suggested that bilingualism (teaching both languages sequentially) is a better method as it celebrates both languages equally. In many countries around the world, such as Luxembourg and the Philippines, bilingual education is the norm for all pupils, while in Canada and New Zealand it is at the request of the parents (Garcia, 2009: 139).

In 2001, Ofsted analysed both approaches in England and discovered that good-quality teaching and learning happened because of good-quality joint working between EAL staff and teachers in mainstream schools. Withdrawal of pupils, which is the UK's custom with bilingual education, was less successful than the provision provided in class.

Withdrawing pupils as a method of bilingual teaching may not, however, always be possible, especially if you have more than one home language in a classroom. In some UK classes there can be (other than English) three or more different languages spoken and so it would not be cost effective or possible to provide this type of bilingual education for each child (Bakhsh, Harding and Vaughan, 1985: 13). For this reason it seems likely that 'Immersion' is the teaching style that you will have no choice but to adopt.

What is the fastest method?

Cummins feels that a person needs total immersion in a language to be able to learn, but how fast they learn depends upon how efficient they are in their mother tongue. He calls this developmental interdependence: the development of the second language is dependent on the first (Cummins, 1979: 222). For example, if a child does not know colours or numbers in their home language then they may have difficulty learning them in English; likewise if they are able to read and write fluently in their home language it shouldn't take long for them to become fluent in English. Similarly, research in the *International Journal of Bilingual Education and Bilingualism* has shown that high expectations from teachers had a positive effect on children's learning, as did proficiency in their home language (August et al., 2008: 110).

Colin Baker claims that the rate of learning a language is affected by social factors and social interaction rather than by proficiency in the mother tongue. Children can be fluent in English if they are proficient in all areas of oracy and literacy (Baker, 2001: 5). Such skills are categorised as listening, speaking, reading and writing. Some of these skills, such as listening and reading, are receptive and some – speaking and writing – productive, yet all need to be taught and learnt in the new language. When a person is proficient in all areas then they are fluent in a language.

To become fluent, learners need opportunities for social interaction and some linguistic input in the language. If the learner does not have opportunities to interact with the language then the rate of fluency is likely to be slower.

How do we support EAL learners in the multilingual classroom?

Baker suggests that there are two routes into fluency: Simultaneous and Sequential. Simultaneous is where a person learns a language whilst learning another, while Sequential is where they learn a language in a formal sequence, i.e. first vocabulary, then grammar etc. They do not learn another language at the same time.

Jim Cummins suggested that English can be taught either sequentially or simultaneously but that children need guidance, especially if the strategy is one of Immersion. He pointed out that children need experience of particular skills, namely BIC and CALP, to be able to become fluent multilingual speakers.

BIC is Basic Interpersonal Communication. This is chatting about things in common, such as TV programmes or sport, and organisational language such as instructions etc.

CALP is Cognitive/Academic Language Proficiency. This is where the learner uses language for reflection, evaluation, analysis, and so on. CALP is the high-order thinking that we are trying to encourage in the classroom.

Figure 1 opposite demonstrates how children learn CALP and BIC skills and has become the agreed way of focusing on how to cognitively develop a child who is learning through the Immersion method.

The framework suggests that to achieve CALP we need to try to provide activities in the B quadrant of Figure 1: context embedded and cognitively demanding. This would mean that a child understands what to do and how to do something but that it is challenging them on an academic and cognitive level.

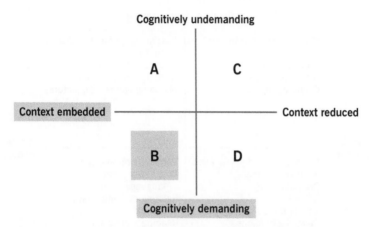

Figure 1: How children learn CALP and BIC skills (Cummins, J., *Language, Power and Pedagogy*, Multilingual Matters Ltd, 2000)

To achieve BIC the learning can be in the A quadrant. Children need experience of both to acquire fluency in a new language. BIC and CALP should be seen as of equal value rather than CALP being the better, more advanced skill. Both need to be used to develop language and each has its own set of skills with their own set of challenges to master.

Many activities in a classroom are actually in quadrant D: context reduced and cognitively demanding, so that the EAL pupil is unable to access the teaching and/or achieve deep learning because they don't understand what to do. The challenge for teachers, therefore, is to provide context when teaching abstract themes. Cummins' and Baker's research suggests that children who are acquiring the language take two to seven years to reach the same level of proficiency as a native English speaker if their work is context embedded. Children who have context-reduced work take on average five to ten years.

How to use Cummins' framework

To be able to support an EAL pupil and to maximise learning, a teacher needs to be sensitive to the cognitive demands of an activity and provide contextual support so that the pupil is aware of what is to be learnt and how to achieve that learning (Baker, 2001: 180). Figure 2 overleaf shows the type of activities that can be classified in each quadrant.

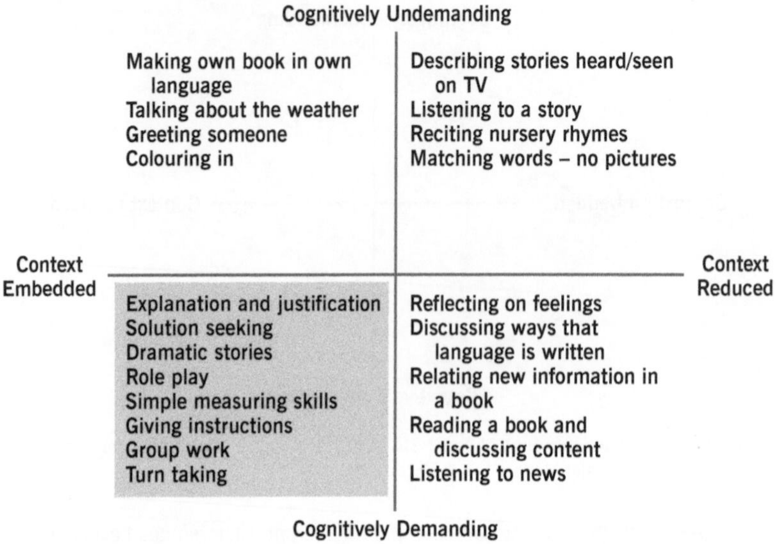

Cognitively Undemanding

Making own book in own language Talking about the weather Greeting someone Colouring in	Describing stories heard/seen on TV Listening to a story Reciting nursery rhymes Matching words – no pictures

Context Embedded ——————————————————————— Context Reduced

Explanation and justification Solution seeking Dramatic stories Role play Simple measuring skills Giving instructions Group work Turn taking	Reflecting on feelings Discussing ways that language is written Relating new information in a book Reading a book and discussing content Listening to news

Cognitively Demanding

Figure 2: How to use Cummins' framework (Baker, C., *Foundations of Bilingual Education and Bilingualism*, 3, Multilingual Matters Ltd, 2001)

Context embedded and cognitively undemanding (A):

- Making their own book in their own language
- Talking about the weather
- Greeting someone
- Colouring familiar pictures
- Drawing the alphabet
- Translating words they already know and producing images to go with them

Context embedded and cognitively demanding (B):

- Explanation and justification
- Solution seeking/problem solving
- Dramatic stories – reading and writing
- Role play
- Simple measuring skills
- Giving instructions
- Small group work
- Turn taking
- Demonstration
- One-to-one work with a teacher or pupil

- Interactive teaching techniques
- Mixed ability groupings
- Discussion
- Jigsaws
- Matching words with pictures and translations
- Word webs about class topic
- Journal writing

Context reduced and cognitively undemanding (C):

- Describing stories
- Listening to a story
- Reciting nursery rhymes
- Matching words without pictures
- Oral explanations
- Worksheets
- Tests/examinations

Context reduced and cognitively demanding (D):

- Reflection
- Discussing ways that language is written
- Relating new information that is read
- Reading a book and discussing content
- Listening to news items
- Matching words
- Spelling tests without definitions
- Definitions of English words without translations
- Interviewing a person or watching an interview
- Tests/examinations

High-order thinking skills such as analysis, synthesis and evaluation are considered to be CALP skills because they use subtle language skills. However, they can be fairly abstract concepts and so we need the teaching and learning to be context embedded so that an EAL pupil can access and develop such skills.

Most if not all learning and teaching should be in quadrant B of Cummins' framework with activities that are understood by the learner but suitably challenging. This can be done through the activities suggested above and within the next chapters of this book. It is best to scaffold learning so that children move from learning with support (quadrant B) to learning without support (quadrant D).

How to ensure learning is context embedded and cognitively demanding

To ensure all learning for EAL pupils is accessible and in quadrant B, it is useful to consider using some of the strategies below in every part of the school day.

Use visual cues

Visual aids can help provide a context for and a visual explanation of what you are teaching. Showing a picture whilst reading something to the class or using the images from a book, or explaining instructions and including a visual format, can support pupils in their comprehension. Consider yourself in a place that speaks a language you are not very familiar with. Think about how you discover where the toilet or bar is (both essentials when on holiday!): a picture usually helps you find things more quickly and without feeling foolish for having to ask somebody. It's the same for an EAL pupil. Visual cues support quicker comprehension.

Be expressive when you teach

Being animated when talking, i.e. using hand gestures and facial expressions, can be a fantastic way to get a message across. If you have ever had experience of trying to work out what someone is trying to say in a different language, you will know that listening to their tone of voice and watching them can help you work out the meaning. This is why it is useful for you to try to bring expression and drama into your teaching. For example, when talking and explaining something, demonstrate what you mean by modelling or using mime. It will not only make your teaching more interesting to watch but will make the learning fun for all your pupils.

Use a bilingual dictionary

There are many inexpensive dual language books available through the internet, but the best text to invest in would be a bilingual dictionary, ideally one that has pictures. Buy one for your pupils (one each) and one for yourself and whenever you need to teach something try to find a few key words that you can put on the board and encourage your EAL pupil to learn. In addition, try to use and speak the key words within your lesson and with the whole class so that your EAL pupil has some understanding of what you are teaching.

Differentiate with mixed-ability groupings

Social interaction is a useful technique that supports all pupils, but EAL pupils in particular. Therefore it is essential that you group your pupils with 'significant others' (Vygotsky, 1978) who have a good level of English. This way the EAL pupil will have a good role model and be able to develop their vocabulary. Mixed-ability groupings can also help more able pupils because they have to explain things to others. This means that their learning is likely to be deep and embedded. Hence mixed-ability grouping is a beneficial technique for all pupils. See below for more details on this area.

Put the EAL pupil in the middle

Whenever you place an EAL pupil in a group of three, ideally of mixed ability, give them the responsibility of the pen and paper and sit them between the two other children. This is so that the native English speakers will talk across the EAL pupil, and so this pupil will listen to language and pick up vocabulary and sentences. Another reason is that the EAL pupil *has* to take part and is in less danger of sitting back and consequently not learning. They are less likely to feel isolated and will, through immersion, understand what to do and what is being learnt.

Talk partners

Having a talk partner is seen as a useful thinking task in most schools, yet for EAL pupils it is essential because it requires the child to use English to communicate thought. An EAL pupil is more likely to talk openly and practise using English if they do not feel under the threat of looking and feeling foolish. With mixed-ability talk partners, an EAL pupil is likely to feel safe and want to share ideas, so it is useful to use talk partners to discuss ideas prior to sharing with the whole class. Also consider using talk partners to reinforce the task that the children are being asked to undertake before they start it. In this way you will be able to see who really understands what to do, and limit the possibility of children getting stuck on their work so you have to explain the task multiple times.

Multiple intelligences

There is a lot of theory about multiple intelligences and it is agreed that intelligence is more than a narrow field (Gardner, 1999). Generally it is important to note that not every child has a specific intelligence and likes to learn in a read-write or auditory manner. The same is true for EAL pupils and so it is useful to ensure that teaching and learning in your classroom use a variety of approaches throughout the year so that children are able to access the curriculum and improve all intelligences. Visual, musical and kinaesthetic intelligences are usually the better methods for EAL pupils, purely because children are able to express what they think in ways that do not always need language that is written or verbal. Occasionally an EAL pupil may find communicating what they know and understand difficult because verbalising and writing is a barrier.

Repetitive language

Using repetitive language and familiar sentences can reinforce a language. So when teaching, reading a book or creating a task try to ensure that there are a set of sentences and/or words that can support the development of vocabulary. Using sentence starters and writing frames can be a scaffold for an EAL pupil which can be removed over time.

Labels

Label everything that you think will be useful for your pupil in their home language – pencils, toilet, rules, safety instructions etc. It is also useful to have the labels in pictorial form.

One-to-one communication

Whenever possible, find time to talk with the EAL pupil(s) in your class. This can be discussion about personal interests or class-related issues. Listening and communicating with you will help your pupil(s) feel valued and begin to develop their vocabulary. During these times try to speak some phrases in their home language such as 'Isn't it a lovely day!' as it will add to their sense of security and interest in learning.

Cultural celebration

Celebrate their language! It seems obvious, but displaying their national flag, listening to music from their homeland and culture, reading and listening to traditional tales from their country/continent can make the children in the rest of the class value the EAL pupil and therefore want to help them learn. As Cummins suggested, it is important that the pupil learning English doesn't forget their home language as each is dependent on the other.

Let them be!

It is important to let EAL pupils have a rest. It is very intense to be immersed in a language and it can be extremely tiring. It is essential therefore to let your pupils be and not insist that they learn English in a formal way all the time they are in school. Their brain is likely to be picking up languages without formal teaching and so it is important that at times you let them **sit**, **watch** and **listen**.

The importance of differentiation (GOTOS)

As I have previously mentioned, mixed-ability groupings are the best learning situations for EAL pupils. Yet, in my experience, many teachers and trainee teachers I have observed and discussed EAL practice with, have put pupils with early stages of English in ability sets, usually the lower reading/writing English ability group.

Differentiation isn't solely about ability and tasks related to it. It is about capability and potential and using various teaching strategies to support learning. Placing an EAL pupil at any of the first three stages mentioned above with native English speakers who have difficulty in learning and grasping the language themselves can hinder their progress. Without good role models and social interaction (Vygotsky, 1978) any task can potentially become a barrier to accessing creative high-order thinking, rich vocabulary and deep learning because the context is reduced and cognitively undemanding. It is essential therefore to think creatively about differentiation. Divide your class into groups that suit the activity and support every child's learning.

Using a mnemonic such as GOTOS (Webster, 2010: 107) can help you support the EAL pupils in your class so that they can address the task and successfully accomplish it to the best of their capability. GOTOS are:

Groupings – choose the best sort of group to support learning, e.g. talk partners, mixed-ability pairs, mixed-ability threes or groups, ability groups or pairs, snowballing into a group, friendship groups or expert groups etc.

Organisation – how to organise your classroom. A child who has behaviour issues may need to be near an adult or you might need to change the classroom around to stage a debate or a large art work etc. Make the classroom environment a form of differentiation so that it doesn't become a barrier to creativity and learning.

Task – differentiation by task. This means a task/activity is planned to suit a specific need for a specific child or group of children, e.g. coloured paper for a dyslexic child or a specific writing tool for a child with a physical need or the use of visual aids etc. for a child with visual learning needs. This may mean you have six different activities that cater for the various needs within the class. Occasionally some needs and abilities may be grouped together but don't assume that there are always three or four different abilities in a class. There are usually more specific needs that should be considered and catered for.

Outcome – this is where the children have the same activity but can complete it at their own competency. The outcome is different for each child but the task is the same.

Staff – a member of staff is designated to support a particular child or group of children. You must say, however, how he/she will be supporting them: e.g. through discussion, writing, reading, or questioning.

I can't stress enough that differentiation and careful planning is the key to successfully supporting a pupil who has English as an additional language.

10 top tips

Teaching EAL pupils can feel daunting, especially if you are unable to speak the different language(s) within your classroom, but here are ten top tips (in no particular order) that should help you. Use them as a guide when planning and you should always be able to support your pupils.

- Buy a dictionary so that you can converse at a basic level and make the pupil feel secure. Make sure that they also have a bilingual (ideally picture) dictionary and encourage your EAL pupil(s) to use it regularly.
- Take time to watch an EAL child at play as this is where you will be able to begin to assess their grasp of English.
- Use visual aids and non-verbal communication in all aspects of the school day and for timetabling, labelling of equipment etc. The barrier for an EAL pupil is usually language, so try to turn abstract ideas into concrete terms.
- Remember to put the EAL pupil(s) into mixed-ability groups until you have effectively assessed their learning capabilities and needs for different subjects. Try not to keep them in one particular ability stream all the time, unless that is what their learning need requires.
- Always consider GOTOS (Groupings, Outcome, Task, Organisation and Staff) for differentiation.
- Place the EAL pupil with children who have a good grasp of spoken English rather than children who speak their home language. They need good role models and social interaction to be able to achieve deep learning. Then place them in the middle of a group of three, with the responsibility of the pen and paper, so that they have no opportunity to withdraw from interacting with other children and from learning.

- Use interactive teaching techniques in all your lessons and daily instructions.
- Always try to plan for 'context embedded' and 'cognitively demanding' work.
- Remember that children need experience of BIC and CALP skills.
- Remember the country/continent they have come from and the cultural differences that may have an impact on understanding British conventions and school systems.

The following chapters are a selection of ideas and activities that should help you support all the pupils in your class but especially the EAL children. They can be used and adapted to suit your learners and within a variety of lessons as a starter or plenary or they can be independent CALP activities. Some activities are created as time fillers and should support BIC rather than CALP.

Chapter 2
First days and weeks:

activities and ideas for when an EAL pupil first arrives in class

Introduction

Ideally we know when we are getting a new pupil in our class and so it's a good idea to have systems in place to welcome them. The activities and ideas in this chapter are designed to help you support the child in their first few days whether you knew they were coming or not.

You will find general tips, lesson ideas and activities that will support you and your EAL pupil. They are designed to encourage a smooth transition into the systems of the class, and some ideas will give you a starting point to help you communicate with your new pupil and enable you to feel confident about addressing the child's emotional and learning needs.

Lost in translation!

> Buying a bilingual dictionary will help the child feel welcome and safe. Dictionary work alongside learning a few phrases in the newly arrived pupil's home language will begin to dispel some of the child's first fears.

Aims

- To help a newly arrived EAL pupil(s) feel accepted and safe
- To help you build a relationship with a newly arrived pupil(s)
- To open a channel of communication and acceptance based on mutual respect
- BIC

Vocabulary

Translations of everyday phrases such as:

    Hello
    Goodbye
    How are you?
    My name is . . .
    Welcome!
    Where is the . . . toilet, pen, drink, food, playground?
    I'm glad you are here!

Resources

- An English picture dictionary
- A bilingual pocket dictionary for you and your newly arrived pupil
- A phrase book that translates helpful sentences such as Hello, Where is the . . . ? How are you? etc. into English and vice versa

What to do

- Start by learning a few set phrases in the child's home language so that when you meet the newly arrived pupil you can immediately build a relationship by using them, for example:
  - Welcome to class X
  - My name is . . .
  - What is your name?
  - X is here to help you today/tomorrow/all the time
  - This is called X in English
- Teach a few key phrases to your class so that they can also welcome the pupil(s).
- Teach your class and EAL pupil(s) how to use an English dictionary and how to use a bilingual dictionary through a game of word bingo (see the next activity 'Bingo!').
- Ask the newly arrived EAL pupil(s) to use the picture dictionary to create their own bilingual version that can be used by other children, you and themselves. This can be completed individually in class, at home with parents or with children in the class. It would be good to laminate the book so that it is robust enough to be handled by many children.

Suitable for

Any Key Stage

Variations

- If your school is teaching a Modern Foreign Language, consider adopting the language of your newly arrived pupil(s) and then the EAL pupil can be your teaching assistant.
- If the child has any books in his/her home language, encourage him/her to bring them into school and put them on display next to the bilingual dictionary for the pupils to use.

Bingo!

Bingo is a popular game in schools and perfect for EAL pupils as it reinforces word recognition and develops vocabulary in a fun way.

Aims

- To develop vocabulary
- BIC

Vocabulary

Any words that relate to the class topic or subject that is being taught
Any high-frequency words that the pupil needs to learn

Resources

- Laminated Bingo grid with words on
- White board markers
- A list of laminated words that you call out for the game
- Dictionaries

What to do

- Provide each mixed-ability pair with a Bingo card and white board marker.
- At a fairly fast pace, call out and hold up a selection of words and show what they mean with a large image.
- The children look at their card and if they have the word that you called out, they colour it with their marker.
- The first pair to colour all of their words or make a line of words (you decide the rule) calls 'BINGO!' or a word related to the learning aim, such as the theme of the topic: 'TUDORS!', 'SCHOOL!' etc.

This can be played in mixed-ability pairs where the EAL pupil shares a Bingo card with a native English speaker, eventually playing with their own individual card when they are more confident.

Suitable for

Any Key Stage

Variations

- You could use your interactive white board to show the words alongside images to reinforce the meaning.
- You could have Bingo cards that show images rather than words. The pupils have to relate what you show to the corresponding word, or vice versa.
- To extend the activity the children could play sentence Bingo: they have sentences on their Bingo cards and you read sentences aloud instead of words.

Buddy

A buddy is a child chosen to befriend the newly arrived pupil and should have a good grasp of spoken English but need not be a gifted and talented pupil.

Aims

- To help the newly arrived EAL pupil feel accepted in the class
- To help the newly arrived pupil feel secure when learning about and understanding the school rules and daily systems
- BIC

Vocabulary

Buddy
Friend
Helper
Toilet
Dinner/lunch
Bell
Home time

Resources

- Paper
- Colouring pencils
- Blu-Tack
- Time

What to do

- Choose a kind, patient and friendly pupil who does not mind looking after a new member of the class and who is able to welcome them into their friendship network. Also make sure your buddy has the same sort of dinner as your EAL pupil, i.e. packed lunch or school dinners, so that they can sit together.

- Give them the title and responsibility of buddy and possibly provide a badge with this title in both English and the home language of the newly arrived EAL pupil, ideally before the pupil arrives in the class.
- Provide a chair next to the buddy for the EAL pupil; together they create a name plate for the pupil's tray and coat.
- Together the buddy and pupil walk around the school and the buddy points out the toilet, playground, cloakroom and dinner hall. They then create a school map that includes English words written by the buddy and home-language words by the EAL pupil.
- At playtime ask the buddy to play some key playground games with the EAL pupil that are repetitive and fun – you may also wish to join in!
- At lunch time the buddy helps the pupil with the systems of collecting dinner (if they are taking school dinners) and/or where to sit if they have brought a packed lunch.
- The last activity is to create a visual account of a typical day at the new school that includes when the bell is rung, what to do for dinner, where to go for playtime etc. This can be created any way the children wish. The EAL pupil can take this home to show his/her family so that they can discuss what they do and encourage family involvement.

Suitable for

Any Key Stage

Variations

- The pupil may wish to create at home a visual representation of their experiences in the last school that they were in and then show this to the class. Only do this if you are confident that the past experiences have not been difficult or harrowing, as may be the case with a refugee pupil. Also only do this if the child is happy and confident about sharing experiences with the new class.
- Remember that the EAL pupil may not know what a fire drill or bell is, so ensure that they are looked after if/when this occurs – no matter how long they have been at the school it's still a shock when it happens for the first time.

Simon helps to survive the system!

A game of 'Simon Says' that encourages the use of language a child will find essential in their first few days in school.

Aims

- To help a newly arrived pupil with EAL gain language that will help them with basic needs
- BIC

Vocabulary

Toilet	Lunch	Happy	Stand up	Go to desk
Pen	Play	Sad	Hands up	Go to tray
Pencil	Football	Quiet	No	Hang up coat
Work	Skip	Sit down	Yes	Sit up
Water	Food	Line up	Sit on the carpet	Heads down

Resources

- 'Simon Says' as a starting sentence on the board so that you can point to it and then add the picture at the end
- Large pictures that represent the English words you are saying, such as toilet, drink

What to do

- Play the game of 'Simon Says' but include actions that will be essential for surviving the first few days in school, such as 'Simon says eat dinner'; 'Simon says go to the toilet'; 'Simon says find your pencil' – the children mime eating dinner etc. Whilst saying the action it is a very good idea to hold up a visual representation of it and stress the word such as *dinner* or *toilet* to aid the pupil's understanding.

- The children only do the action if Simon says it. If the phrase 'Simon Says' does not start the sentence then they do not do the action, they stand still. If they do the action when you did not start the sentence with 'Simon Says' then they are out and sit down and watch the rest of the class until there is one child left standing.
- Demonstrate how the game works before you do it with the whole class so that the EAL pupil can see how it is played and learn the rules through the visual aids you provide and the responses of his/ her new classmates.
- When you involve the EAL pupil in the game for the first few times always point to the Simon Says phrase on the board so that they grasp your visual clue. Once you feel they understand the basic rules and recognise this phrase, stop doing this.

Suitable for

KS1, KS2

Variations

- It might be an idea to do this game in pairs so that your new pupil can have his/her buddy as a support before moving on to doing this activity individually.

School systems

> This is a good way of enabling an EAL pupil to develop the basic vocabulary that is associated with school and the classroom. This activity can be completed independently but is more fun if done in a pair.

Aims

- To widen basic vocabulary
- To feel more at home in the school environment
- To be able to name parts of the school environment
- BIC

Vocabulary

The child chooses the vocabulary they wish to use by choosing what to label.

Resources

- Blu-Tack
- Post-it notes
- Paper
- Laminator
- Coloured pens
- Picture dictionary/bilingual dictionary

What to do

- With a buddy encourage the EAL pupil(s) to walk around the classroom and (using a Post-it note) write the English and home language names of different parts of the room and objects that are contained in it. They then stick the Post-it on the object, e.g. chair or part of the room, such as window, and write it in English *and* their home language. If they don't know it in English then they ask their buddy and/or use a dictionary.

- Once they have done this, encourage them to create bilingual labels for selective parts of the room and objects. They should make these colourful and laminate them so that they can become part of the classroom display.

Suitable for

KS1, KS2

Variations

- This can be extended into the whole of the school, and also the creation of the laminated labels can become a class rather than a small group/ individual activity.

Singing solutions!

A fun action song that can help pupils learn basic vocabulary and can be adapted to include new vocabulary lists.

Aims

- To learn the names of body parts in English and in the home language of the EAL pupil(s)
- To sing and enjoy learning together as a class
- To build a sense of class community to help the newly arrived pupil(s) settle in
- BIC

Vocabulary

Head	Nod	Mouth
Shoulders	Thumb	Nose
Knees	Finger	Ear
Toes	Eye	

Resources

- Voice (you may have a piano but it's not always necessary)

What to do

- Sing 'Heads, Shoulders, Knees and Toes' and practise the movements and song (see Appendix 1).
- Eventually you will hum the whole song, but continue with touching the body parts and then finally sing the whole song with all the words and actions as an ending to the activity.

Suitable for

KS1; yet variations would suit KS2

Variations

- Replace the English words for head, shoulders, knees, toes, eye, ear, mouth and nose with a translation from the home language. Sing the song again but with the new translations inserted into the English sentences.
- Use the same tune but choose your own vocabulary list, such as objects in the classroom, food items, friends or mathematical objects.

> *Chair, table, door and drink, door and drink*
> *Chair, table, door and drink, door and drink*
> *Window, floor, pen and ceiling with light*
> *Chair, table, door and drink, door and drink*

Find a name!

 A fun activity that encourages children to learn particular words.

Aims

- To help children learn the names of animals
- To work cooperatively and build relationships
- To develop vocabulary
- BIC

Vocabulary

Names of animals

Resources

- Pictures of animals to hang around necks
- Name cards of the animals

What to do

- Provide each child with an image of an animal to place on their chest. It can be hung like a necklace.
- Give out corresponding word cards and tell the class that they have 30 seconds to find the child with the image of the animal that is listed on their card.
- They then work with this partner or try another set of cards.

Suitable for

Any Key Stage as an introduction activity to a particular lesson

Variations

- This can be done with the children's names rather than image cards, or with the names of science equipment etc.

Find someone who . . .

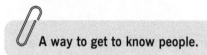

A way to get to know people.

Aims

- To get to know a class of pupils and find commonalities
- To work cooperatively and build relationships
- To develop confidence to ask two basic questions
- BIC

Vocabulary

Language related to hobbies, interests, likes/dislikes

Resources:

- Large hall

What to do

- Give the children a set of questions to ask each other to find out things they have in common. For example:
  - What football team do you like?
  - What letter does your name begin with?
  - What sort of music do you like?
  - Where did you go on holiday?
- The pupils walk around the room and find someone who has two things in common with them, who then becomes their partner.

Suitable for

Any Key Stage

Variations

None

What's my present?

A simple game that encourages watching and describing simple actions.

Aims

- To develop confidence to describe a simple action
- To work cooperatively and build relationships
- To become part of a class
- To be imaginative
- BIC

Vocabulary

Mime
Present
Gift

Resources

- Large hall

What to do

- The children sit in a large circle and pass around an imaginary box. As the box passes from one child to another it can change size.
- Each child has to mime opening the box and then mime what is inside it, such as a scarf, a pet, a ring etc.
- The rest of the class have three chances to guess what it is.

Suitable for

Any Key Stage

Variations

None

Mirror, mirror

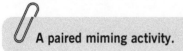 A paired miming activity.

Aims

- To get to know a child from the class and work with them
- To work cooperatively and build relationships
- To be creative
- BIC

Vocabulary

Mime

Resources

- Large hall

What to do

- Pair the pupils so that they are facing each other.
- Explain that they are to mime each other's facial expressions. One child is a mirror whereas the other is its reflection.
- Change partners after a while.

Suitable for

Any Key Stage

Variations

None

This is the word!

A fun activity that encourages drama based on a selection of sentences.

Aims

- To work as a team
- To work cooperatively and build relationships
- To develop some basic understanding of how sentences have meaning
- BIC

Vocabulary

Basic sentences such as:

> He walked slowly.
> She skipped and hugged her friend.
> He was angry with her.
> She cried.

Resources

- Packs of sentences

What to do

- Organise the class into mixed-ability groups of about four.
- Give each group a pack of 4–8 simple random sentences.
- They have to put these sentences in some form of order and act out a story based on them.
- The rest of the class give feedback on whether it made sense or not.

Suitable for

Any Key Stage

Variations

Give one sentence to each group, who then have to act it out without saying it. The rest of the class work out what the sentence was.

Express yourself!

> A short activity that encourages improvisation and intonation in spoken English.

Aims

- To work cooperatively and build relationships
- To develop some basic understanding of how sentences have meaning and can be expressed differently
- BIC

Vocabulary

Basic sentences such as:

More tea, Vicar?
I love you!
I hate your shoes!
I feel sad!
I feel happy!

Expression: emphatically, slowly, sadly, desperately, lonely

Resources

- Basic sentences

What to do

- The class sit or stand in a circle and you provide them with a sentence that they have to repeat, such as 'I love you!'
- Taking turns around the circle, each child has to express it differently, such as emphatically, slowly, sadly, desperately etc. – they choose how to say it.
- After a few children have shown how to say it in various ways, change the sentence for the rest of the class.

Suitable for

Any Key Stage

Variations

The children act out the expression at the same time.

Who's who?

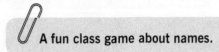

A fun class game about names.

Aims

- To help children learn the names of the class and reinforce the alphabet
- To work cooperatively and build relationships
- To develop vocabulary
- BIC

Vocabulary

Names of children
The alphabet and words related to it

Resources

- Large hall

What to do

- The children stand in a large circle facing each other.
- The first child in the circle says a sentence and links their name to an animal and then makes an action and sound like that animal, e.g. 'Hi, my name is Arjun and I like apes – Ooo! Ooo!' 'Hi, my name is Maggie and I like mice – eek! eek!'
- The rest of the class copy the actions and repeat the child's sentence.

Suitable for

Any Key Stage

Variations

This can be used for what the children like and dislike.

Chapter 3
Activities and ideas for social and cultural integration

Introduction

This chapter has a selection of fun ideas and activities that use repetitive language, easy to follow instructions and team work. They are useful for helping EAL pupils socialise and integrate with their peers, which can be difficult at times.

Many of the activities and ideas are song-based because they use repetitive language and kinaesthetic and musical intelligences, which are some of the most suitable ways to support EAL pupils in school (see Chapter 1). The songs can be adapted to suit the needs of your class and Key Stage.

Playground games

These activities involve a group of children but can be taught to the whole class. They encourage the development of vocabulary and general sentence structure through team work and a sense of fun. It is advisable for a teacher to teach the traditional games to the class, especially when the EAL pupil is new to the school, so that they can eventually play them independently from an adult.

Indoor play games and activities

Play time in the UK is at times naturally indoors and so these activities can be conducted independently or in small groups. The ideas encourage language acquisition through repetitive word and sentence games.

Routines and codes of behaviour

The ideas in this section offer children a safe and fun way into understanding the class and school routines and they encourage celebration of the cultural similarities and differences of the pupils' home lives.

Playground games

Parachute!

A fun class activity that can be played in the hall or outside which reinforces high-frequency words.

Aims

- To recognise and build up key vocabulary
- To develop a sense of team work and class friendship
- BIC/CALP

Vocabulary

Quickly
Slowly
Smoothly
Initial letters – alphabet
Colours
Names of the parts of a classroom (window, door, floor, ceiling, chair)

Resources

- A large nylon parachute (can be bought from large supermarkets or school purchasing catalogues)

What to do

- Each child holds a small area of the parachute and the class move their arms up and down so that the parachute makes waves. Instruct the class to 'Move the parachute . . . quickly/slowly/smoothly'.
- The next activity is for the children to move under the parachute when you say the name of an animal in the UK or a part of the classroom that begins with the initial letter of their name. They run under the parachute and change places with another. Do this a few times but vary it by saying it's the last letter of their own name or the name of their buddy etc.

- In the next word activity give each child the name of a colour, plant, animal or part of the classroom such as window, door etc. (anything the EAL pupil needs to know the name of). Only choose four or five words and go round the circle so that there are about four children who have the same word. Inform the class that when you say their new name they have to let go of the parachute and run underneath, changing places with each other. Also tell them that when you shout the collective noun such as Colour! Plant! Classroom! all the children have to let go of the parachute and change places. They must try to pick the parachute up quickly and carry on waving before it blows away.
- To end this parachute activity ask the class to move the parachute, then, after counting three, to wave the parachute high in the air then quickly bring it down and tuck it under their bottom so that they sit inside the tent. In this space you can do circle time and ask each child one thing they like about using a parachute and why. Use a repetitive sentence such as 'I liked the parachute because . . .'

Suitable for

Any Key Stage

Variations

- This activity can be adapted by introducing a ball and trying to get it to move clockwise then anticlockwise; by developing a sentence such as 'I ran under the parachute and I touched Jamie'; or by showing a card with a word on rather than shouting it, so that the children have to read the word and recognise it before running underneath the parachute.

'Oranges and Lemons'

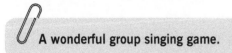

A wonderful group singing game.

Aims

- To recognise and build up key vocabulary from repetitive sentences
- To develop a sense of class friendship
- BIC

Vocabulary

The song 'Oranges and Lemons' (see Appendix 1)

Resources

None

What to do

- In teams of no more than ten, two children (one could be you) stand facing each other with about a foot gap, with their arms raised. They touch their hands and clasp fingers so that they look like a bridge.
- The rest of the class slowly take turns to walk, skip, jump under the hands and gaps whilst singing the song 'Oranges and Lemons' (see Appendix 1).
- When the song reaches the climax and the final line, the hands come down and trap whoever is under the 'bridge' at the time. They become the bridge and the children repeat the song and activity.

Suitable for

KS1, KS2

'Ring a Ring of Roses'

A traditional circle game where the children link hands and skip in a circle whilst singing the song.

Aims

- To recognise and build up key vocabulary from repetitive sentences
- To develop a sense of class friendship
- BIC

Vocabulary

The rhyme 'Ring a Ring of Roses' (see Appendix 1)

Resources

None

What to do

- The children hold hands so that they form a circle and move in a clockwise direction whilst saying the rhyme. They fall to the ground and pretend to sneeze when they say *Atishoo, atishoo, we all fall down*.

Suitable for

KS1

Variations

- There are variations of this rhyme: http://www.kididdles.com/lyrics/r035.html is a good place to start.
- Children can also make up their own actions for each part.

'Teddy Bear'

A fun skipping game where two children turn a large rope and the rest take turns to skip in the centre and do the actions of the song without getting caught on the rope.

Aims

- To build up an understanding of vocabulary associated with actions from repetitive sentences
- To develop a sense of class friendship
- BIC

Vocabulary

Repetitive rhyme 'Teddy Bear' (see Appendix 1)

Resources

- Large skipping rope

What to do

- Two children turn the rope and the rest take it in turns to jump into the turning rope. Whilst the class are chanting the rhyme the child does the actions.

  Teddy bear Teddy bear

  Turn around (They turn around and jump at the same time)

  Touch the ground (They touch the floor and carry on jumping)

  Touch your shoe (They touch their shoe whilst jumping)

  That will do! (They look sulky with hands on hips)

  Switch off the light (They mime switching off a light whilst jumping)

  Say good-night! (They bow or say good-night and then leave the skipping area)

  (See Appendix 1)

- If they stop the rope and don't manage to do the actions and jump they take over from someone who is turning the rope and that person joins the jumping queue.

Suitable for

KS1, KS2

Variations

- You could make up a new rhyme with actions about school, for instance.
- Two children could jump simultaneously in the large rope.
- You could skip with them!

'Miss Susie had a Baby!'

A fun skipping game with a large group of children who enter the rope as the song develops so that eventually there are five children skipping simultaneously.

Aims

- To build up an understanding of vocabulary associated with actions from repetitive sentences
- To develop a sense of class friendship
- BIC

Vocabulary

The song 'Miss Susie had a Baby!' (see Appendix 1)

Resources

Large skipping rope

What to do

- Two children (you could be one of them) turn the long rope whilst the rest line up at the side of the rope.
- One child ('Susie') jumps in and everyone starts to sing (see Appendix 1). When they get to the fourth verse,
  In came the doctor,
  In came the nurse,
  In came the lady,
  With the alligator purse
  new children enter the jumping area and jump rope with 'Susie'.
- When the class sing the final verse the 'doctor' and 'nurse' leave the area and only 'Susie' and 'the lady' remain, shaking hands.
  Miss Susie punched the doctor,
  Miss Susie kicked the nurse,
  Miss Susie thanked the lady
  With the alligator purse
- When the song is finished it is repeated with new people.

Suitable for

KS1, KS2

Variations

- No variations but there are many other versions of this song and occasionally it is chanted rather than sung. There are no penalties for stopping the rope but you could introduce some new rules such as a person who stops the rope has to go back in the queue and the next in line jumps the rope instead.

'The Farmer's in the Dell'

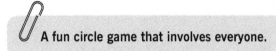

A fun circle game that involves everyone.

Aims

- To build up an understanding of vocabulary associated with farm animals and family
- To develop a sense of class friendship
- BIC

Vocabulary

The song 'The Farmer's in the Dell' (see Appendix 1)

> 1. *The farmer's in the dell, the farmer's in the dell*
>   *Ee-i-ad-eo*
>   *The farmer's in the dell!*

Next verses . . .

> 2. *The farmer wants a wife*
> 3. *The wife wants a child*
> 4. *The child wants a dog*
> 5. *We all pat the dog*

Resources

None

What to do

- The children hold hands in a large circle and one child is chosen to be the farmer and stands in the centre. The class slowly move around the farmer in a clockwise direction and sing the first two verses of the song (see Appendix 1).
- At the end of the second verse, 'The farmer wants a wife', the 'farmer' chooses a child to be his/her 'wife' and they enter the circle. The tune is sung again with the third verse, 'The wife wants a child', and at the end the 'wife' chooses someone.

- The tune is sung with the fourth verse, 'The child wants a dog', and the 'child' chooses a dog.
- The final verse is sung, but this time the large group close in and pat the 'dog' at the same time.
- When you have sung it through once you can repeat the song with different children.

Suitable for

KS1

Variations

- You can include other verses/sentences such as
  The dog wants a cat
  The cat wants a mouse
  The mouse eats his cheese
- You could create your own version based on the names of the children in the class.

'What's the time, Mr Wolf?'

> A fun group game that involves running and learning a little about the vocabulary of time.

Aims

- To learn vocabulary associated with time
- To develop a sense of class friendship
- BIC/CALP

Vocabulary

Repetitive sentence, 'What's the time, Mr Wolf?'
Vocabulary related to time such as half past, quarter past, o'clock
Numbers

Resources

None (however, see Variations)

What to do

- One child is 'Mr Wolf' (this can be you) and has their back to the rest of the group, who are lined up at quite a distance away.
- The group chant *What's the time, Mr Wolf?* whilst taking large steps and walking slowly towards 'Mr Wolf'.
- Mr Wolf turns and says a time to the group.
- This is repeated and the group move closer to Mr Wolf. The aim is to get to where he/she stands before being touched by him/her.
- However, whenever Mr Wolf wants to, he/she can turn after the question and shout 'DINNER TIME!' When this happens, Mr Wolf runs after the group and aims to catch one of them. If they are caught they then become the next Mr Wolf or sit out until all the group are caught (depending on your rules and how cold it is outside).

Suitable for

KS1

Variations

- Use a demonstration clock and/or flash cards with the group so they can see the time you are saying as well as hear it.

Stuck in the mud!

A fun class activity that involves lots of team work and running about.

Aims

- To recognise and build up key playground and survival vocabulary
- To develop a sense of team work and class friendship based on mutual respect
- BIC

Vocabulary

Language associated with the game such as:
Mud
'You're it'
Run!
Quick!
'You're free'
Arms
Legs

Resources

None necessary, but bands could be used to distinguish between team members.

What to do

- Two, three or four children are the 'it' team and have to chase the rest of the group and touch them. The aim is to get as many of the other team stuck (standing still) as possible.
- If a child is touched by one who is 'it' then they have to stand still with their arms and legs astride. They are stuck in that position until a member of their own team reaches them and climbs under their legs or under their arms. Once they do this the child is free to run around again and avoid being tagged by the team that is 'it'.
- If they are tagged by an 'it' team member whilst trying to free another then they are also stuck in the mud.

Suitable for

KS1, KS2

Variations

- This is a variation of Tag, but you can add new rules such as if you are stuck for more than a minute you have to become an 'it' team member.

Duck, duck, goose!

A funny game that takes children by surprise.

Aims

- To recognise and build up key playground and survival vocabulary
- To develop a sense of team work and class friendship based on mutual respect
- BIC

Vocabulary

Playground language such as: Run! This isn't your space! Quick! Well done!
Duck! Goose!

Resources

None

What to do

- The children stand or sit in a large circle and one child is on the
  outside of the circle walking in a clockwise direction.
- They touch each person and each time say 'duck'.
- When they feel like it they touch someone and say 'goose' – they
  then start to run in a clockwise direction.
- The 'goose' runs in an anticlockwise direction and the aim is to get
  back to the gap they left in the circle.
- Whoever gets to the place first stays and the person on the outside
  has to go around saying 'duck' until they find a 'goose' they wish to
  run against.

Suitable for

KS1, KS2

Variations

- You can have more than one person tapping 'duck' at the same time. It can be more fun this way although a little confusing at times.
- You could change the words from duck and goose to ones that are more relevant to your class.

'Who took the cookie?'

A quick clapping and chanting game that uses repetitive rhyme – a good start to getting the children ready for playtime.

Aims

- To practise language associated with denials and questions using repetitive sentences
- To practise tone in language
- BIC

Vocabulary

The cookie rhyme:
Group: *Who took the cookie from the cookie jar?*
Teacher: *Faisal took the cookie from the cookie jar!*
Faisal: *Who me?*
Group: *Yes you!*
Faisal: *Couldn't be!*
Group: *Then who?*
Faisal: *Jacob took the cookie from the cookie jar!*
Jacob: *Who me?*
etc.

Resources

None

What to do

- The children clap the rhythm on their lap and hands when they are chanting this rhyme.
- Teacher starts the rhyme off by choosing a child. Teacher: *Faisal took the cookie from the cookie jar!* And then this chant is carried on until everyone has had a go or it is playtime.

Suitable for

KS1, KS2

Variations

There are many other class clapping chants that have a similar aim such as:

- 'The Telephone Song'. See Appendix 1.
- 'Queenie I'. A child is chosen as leader and they go out the room. A ball or something else is hidden in a child's hand and then placed behind his/her back. A group of children are chosen to stand at the front with the first child and they put their hands behind their backs for the leader to choose. The leader enters the room and the group start the clapping chant (see Appendix 1).

Indoor play games and activities

Snakes and ladders

A board game that uses turn-taking and language associated with games.

Aims

- To cooperate and be a fair team player
- Developing turn-taking, language and numbers
- BIC/CALP

Vocabulary

Language associated with turn-taking: your turn, my turn, next, down the snake, up the ladder, roll, count, move, counter
Numerical language

Resources

- Snakes and ladders board (either bought or created)
- Dice
- Counters
- Set of question cards for the variation elements

What to do

- This is the traditional game of snakes and ladders. When a child lands on a ladder they move up the ladder onto a new square and if they land on a snake they move down. The aim of the game is to get to the end of the board and reach the final square.
- The players need to roll a six to be able to move their counter onto the board.

Suitable for

Any Key Stage

Variations

- To make this game more language-specific include a set of question cards such as spelling or matching cards (depending on the level of language acquisition your pupils have). When a child lands on a ladder or snake they have to have a card read to them or they read it themselves. If they are correct they move up the ladder, if incorrect they stay where they are. Likewise, if they land on a snake and get the question wrong they move down the snake and if correct they stay where they are. Suggestions for the question cards could be:
  - Spelling activities: consonant, vowel, consonant (CVC) words to more complex phonemes
  - Definition: show a picture/word and the child has to say what it is called in English and/or explain what it is
  - A question related to the topic they are studying

Matching jigsaw

A jigsaw activity that includes matching words/sentences to pictures.

Aims

- To be able to define and translate specific English words
- To begin to structure simple sentences
- To encourage the creation of more complex sentences
- BIC/CALP

Vocabulary

High-frequency words
Vocabulary of the classroom
Topic vocabulary

Resources

- Jigsaw
- Bilingual dictionary

What to do

These jigsaw activities can be made by you and the children or bought from a publisher.

- Make a few rectangles and write on them a selection of words. Use a clip art picture that shows what each word means, such as dog, door, window, desk etc. Laminate the cards.
- Cut each rectangle in half so that the word is on one half and the image on the other half.
- The children match as many of the words as possible to the images. Try to have at least 20 words to match.

The children can do this independently or in pairs.

Suitable for

KS1, KS2

Variations

- One half of the jigsaw will be the start of a sentence and the other half could contain a noun that is associated with the classroom or a picture of that noun, e.g. the teacher sat on the **desk**; the child looked out of the **window**, etc.
- You could also include words that are specific to their topic.
- Consider extending to create an activity where they have to label a diagram or image such as parts of the human body; skeleton; parts of a house etc.

Language Snap!

This activity is based on the original card game 'Snap!' but uses specific language associated with the class topic or basic language that an EAL pupil may need to know over the coming weeks.

Aims

- To enable the EAL pupil to recognise new vocabulary
- To develop their vocabulary in English and translate it into their home language
- To reinforce vocabulary that will be useful in classroom situations
- BIC/CALP

Vocabulary

Any vocabulary associated with the class topic or a specific subject
Any vocabulary that the child may need, such as door, table, parts of the body, colours, numbers etc.
Translations of the chosen vocabulary list into the child's home language

Resources

- Card
- Pictures
- Various coloured pens
- Bilingual dictionary
- Smart board

What to do

- Assess what the EAL pupil's language needs are and create a list of words that they should know and which will be useful to them in class or the playground or in a specific subject such as mathematics.

- Cut up 50 cards (5cm x 5cm) and write (or print using a PC and printer) the words you think will be useful on 25 of the cards and then repeat these on the other 25. It would be useful for your EAL pupil to have a few decks of 'Snap!' cards, each with a different language focus, such as a deck for topic work, a deck for technical language associated with poetry, a deck for Geography or Religious Education etc.
- With an able reader and a clear English speaker the EAL pupil takes 25 cards from the deck of 50 mixed-up cards and their partner has the other 25. They take it in turns to place a card face up in between them, and say aloud the word that is on the card. They do this until two of the cards show the same word, then they have to say the word and then shout 'SNAP!' at the same time as placing their hand over the pile.
- The child who said the word and shouted 'Snap!' first and placed their hand over the pile wins the cards and the game continues until all 50 cards have been dealt and used. The child with the largest hand at the end wins the game.

The child can match the cards alone – however, they will not be able to hear the pronunciation which is important to language acquisition and it isn't so much fun. The more they do this activity the quicker they will be able to recognise a word that has been written or is spoken and develop personal vocabulary that will be useful to them in a classroom situation.

Suitable for

KS1, KS2

Variations

- To make this more complex, create 25 cards that are English words and 25 cards that translate the word into the child's home language. The pupil then plays 'Snap!' but matches the translations.
- The EAL pupil creates their own version of a 'Snap!' game using either card or smart board technology.

Happy Families

This is a card game for two to four individual players or four sets of pairs. The game encourages basic reading and the asking and answering of a repeated question.

Aims

- To interact with peers and build social skills
- To learn basic language structure
- BIC

Vocabulary

Language related to relationships: mother, father, sister, brother etc.
Language related to titles: Mr, Mrs, Master, Miss
Sentence structure related to basic questioning:

Do you have . . .?
Sorry, no, I do not have . . .
Yes I do have . . . here it is.
I have a family set! They are . . .
Thank you!

Resources

- Happy Families card game (52 cards)
- You can buy the cards from **www.amazon.co.uk** or you may wish to make your own (see Variations below)

What to do

- Shuffle the cards and then divide them between the children who are playing. They do not show each other their cards. It may be useful for the EAL pupil to be paired with an able English speaker so that they can quickly learn how to play the game and pick up the language and repetitive sentences in a way that doesn't feel too threatening at first.

- The aim of the game is to make as many family sets as possible. The children take it in turns to ask each other (using a full sentence) if they have a particular card, e.g. 'Do you have Mr Chalk?' If the child on their left does have the card they have to give it to the child who requested it. This continues in a clockwise direction so that each child has the opportunity to ask the child on their left for family cards that they need. When a child has made a family set they place them on the table face up. The first child to have created the most family sets wins the game.

Suitable for

KS1, KS2

Variations

- You could make a 'Happy Families' card game based on your current topic or using objectives from a specific subject: for example, in Science you could have a family of planets, a family of invertebrates/vertebrates, a family of habitats etc; in Religious Education a family of religions or religious festivals or religious symbols or religious leaders; and in Geography a family of continents and countries or weather symbols etc.
- The children could make their own 'Happy Families' game based on an interest such as football.

Word search

> A word search isn't always considered to be of high educational value. However, it does have a place as a wet playtime activity that develops knowledge of vocabulary and spelling. It is also an activity that children seem to enjoy. It can be completed individually or in pairs.

Aims

- To recognise high-frequency words
- To enable the EAL pupil to recognise new vocabulary by sight
- BIC

Vocabulary

Any vocabulary associated with the class topic or a specific subject
Any high-frequency words and vocabulary that the child may need, such as door, table, parts of the body, colours, numbers, 'thank you' etc.

Resources

- A bank of word searches that can either be put into a book or individually laminated and used over and over again with a white board pen.

What to do

- Assess what the EAL pupil's language needs are and create a list of words that they should know and which will be useful to them in class or the playground or in a specific subject such as Science.
- Create a grid that has 20 x 20 squares (each square is 1 or 2cm) and select 10 words that can be placed randomly in the grid; one letter per square. Remember to place some words backwards or diagonally.
- Once you have placed the 10 words fill in the empty blanks with randomly selected letters until each square has a letter and the grid is filled in. List the 10 words that the child needs to find at the bottom of the grid.
- The pupil then looks for the words, which are now hidden, within the grid and once they find them they circle the word and say it aloud.

Suitable for

Any Key Stage

Variations

- The children could make their own English vocabulary word search or one in their home language for their topic.
- You could extend this activity by asking the child, once they have found the words and completed the word search, to find out what each word means.

Crossword

We are all very familiar with crosswords in newspapers, and how they can help with understanding definitions of words and lateral thinking.

Aims

- To develop vocabulary
- To improve dictionary skills
- BIC/CALP

Vocabulary

Language related to class topic, which is reflected in the crossword

Resources

- A bank of laminated crosswords
- A crossword book
- A bilingual dictionary
- A selection of English dictionaries and dictionaries that reflect the various languages in the class

What to do

Having a crossword book is always a useful indoor playtime activity for all children but specifically for an EAL pupil as it encourages the development of vocabulary.

- Create a selection of crossword puzzles that relate to the class topic or a specific subject and laminate them so that they can be reused. Ensure that some crosswords have simple definitions and some contain more difficult cryptic clues so that once a pupil has a good grasp of English they can challenge themselves a little more.
- The pupils try to complete the puzzles using a dry marker.
- The EAL pupil can work individually, or with a partner who has a good grasp of oral and written English and/or use dictionaries to help.

Suitable for

Any Key Stage

Variations

- Buy a selection of crossword books that are designed for children and have them readily available for children to use and complete.
- Extend the activity so that any new word that a child comes across in the crossword is copied onto a piece of paper with its definition and then displayed on a class word wall.

Story tapes

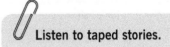

Listen to taped stories.

Aims

- To encourage sentence recognition and vocabulary development
- To listen to a story in English and begin to recognise story or poetry structure
- BIC/CALP

Vocabulary

Any language that is repeated and related to the chosen text
Repetitive rhythm/rhyme in sentences/poetry

Resources

- Tape recorder or iPod and iPod docking station
- Headphones that connect to the listening device
- A selection of story tapes with accompanying book (it would be useful if the book is a dual language book or a book that is written in their home language while the story tape is in English, but this is not essential)
- A selection of poetry tapes with accompanying anthology
- A selection of song tapes with lyrics
- There are many taped stories suitable for children that can be bought from bookshops or can be downloaded from iTunes (http://www.apple.com/itunes) or Amazon (www.amazon.co.uk).

What to do

- Set up a listening area in the classroom and have a number of headphones available so that more than one child can listen simultaneously. Include a selection of story tapes with accompanying texts in pre-organised bags which have large images (rather than text) on the front to show what the book is about.

- The children choose their own story and listen. If they listen in pairs they will then be more likely to discuss it. It is also a good idea for you to discuss the story with the child after they have listened so that they realise that listening to a story usually encourages personal opinion which is worth sharing.
- Some children become confused with so much choice and so in this instance it might be helpful to have the listening area already organised with a tape that is in the machine and ready to be listened to.

Suitable for

KS1, KS2

Variations

- Once the children are aware of what a story tape is, arrange for the pupil to create their own story tape by either reading an existing story onto a Podcast or CD through the use of computer software or by creating their own story with accompanying book and then reading it onto a CD or Podcast to include in the listening library of the school/class for others to enjoy.
- You may also wish to include the child's parents and ask them to record a traditional story in the child's home language which can also be included in the school's/class's listening library.
- There are some stories that are spoken in the child's home language and are great to listen to, especially when the text includes both English and the child's home language.

Routines and codes
of behaviour

Registration

> The children register themselves into and out of class every day.

Aims

- To understand systems within the school day
- To recognise the names of classmates
- BIC

Vocabulary

Names of the children in the class

Resources

- Velcro
- Laminating pouches
- Laminator
- Colours for making name plate
- Card
- Digital camera and photo paper
- Printer

What to do

- Ask the children in the class at the start of the year to create their own name plate, then laminate it and fix Velcro on the back. If an EAL pupil enters mid-year then this is one of the first activities that they do.
- Take a photograph of each child and then make a display of their name plates and faces so that on one side of the display is a photo and on the other a name.

- When the children enter the class at the start of the day they move their name so that it is next to their face. It stays on the display with Velcro. They do the reverse at the end of the day.

Suitable for

KS1, KS2

Variations

You could give this responsibility to the EAL pupil so that they move every child's name, not just their own.

Take me home

The children name a class mascot and then take it home at the weekend and on school holidays.

Aims

- To help pupils become established members of the class and share cultures and interests
- To create a visual representation of what they do in their free time
- BIC/CALP

Vocabulary

Language related to leisure, time and family

Resources

- A soft toy (or class pet)
- A digital camera
- Paper
- Writing/drawing equipment

What to do

- The children take it in turns to take the class mascot home with them on a weekend. They are also given resources such as a camera and paper/pens etc.
- When at home, the child (with members of their family) will take photos, draw and write what the mascot did so that they create a montage of images and if possible words and sentences etc. This will be shown to the class on the Tuesday or in a 'show and tell' session.
- If they do not have a PC at home they can be given time on one Monday to print the images and turn them into a poster or presentation with support from a teaching assistant, another child or yourself.

Suitable for

KS1, KS2

Variations

- They could write words/sentences in their home language to explain what is happening instead of or included with the English.
- Alternatively (if permitted by your health and safety officer) you could have a class pet and do the same activities as with the soft toy.
- Create a diary as if it is written by the mascot with each entry from a different child. Drawings rather than digital images would be included.

All about me!

This idea is based on the 'Children Just Like Me' series. Each of your pupils will create a page about themselves.

Aims

- To share and celebrate similarities and differences in cultures and lifestyles within a class
- To create basic descriptive sentences
- To develop descriptive vocabulary
- BIC/CALP

Vocabulary

Language that describes who they are and what they think:
'This is me'
'I have . . .'
'This is my . . .'
'I like . . . because . . .'
'This is my favourite . . .'
'I live . . .'
'I live with . . .'
'I am from . . .'

Resources

- PC
- Digital camera
- Pens
- Paper
- Scanner
- Glue
- Scissors
- Bilingual dictionary
- Spiral binder and binding

What to do

- Look through the book *Children Just Like Me: A Unique Celebration of Children around the World* by Barnabas and Anabel Kindersley with the class and highlight some of the things the children in the book say about themselves. Show how the information is displayed with a mixture of photos, drawings, information and labelling. It would be good if you created a page about yourself to show how you have taken the basic idea and developed it to show the class all about you.
- Ask the children to design their own page. Encourage them to take photos of at least five items that are personal to them and/or their culture. Explain that these will be included on their personal page. The photographs can be taken at home or the items brought into school and taken in class.
- The children then write a paragraph about themselves that is included on the page. This can be in their home language or English and, if possible, could be translated so that it is a dual language page.
- Once the page is complete, scan it so that it is digitised and then print it using coloured ink. Place the children's pages together and then bind them into a class book using spiral binding.
- Place the book in the class and/or school library to be looked at during reading time or indoor playtime.

Suitable for

Any Key Stage

Variations

- You could create this book using PowerPoint software instead of hard copy. Each child would have a slide which would be put onto a CD and placed in the school library. You could extend this activity to create a Podcast to go with the CD.
- Create a Beebo page or a web page through a safe environment called CEOP (http://www.thinkuknow.co.uk)

Rights and responsibilities

At the start of a new year teachers usually create class rules and write a class agreement. This activity is the same but encourages a more visual representation of the rules.

Aims

- To help the children understand the systems and rules of the class and school
- To work as a team
- BIC/CALP

Vocabulary

'I have . . .'
'I must . . .'
'I have the right to . . .'
'I have the responsibility to . . .'

Resources

- Paper
- Pens
- A selection of art materials

What to do

- In mixed-ability groups of three (with the EAL pupil sitting in the centre of the three) the children list the Rights they think they are entitled to in the classroom, such as 'I have the Right to go to the toilet when I need to'.
- Share the ideas with the class and then ask the groups to go back to their Rights and think of a Responsibility that goes with each one. For example: 'I have a Right to learn', so the Responsibility would be 'I have the Responsibility to take an active part in lessons'.

- Then as a class through a democratic voting system (you could do 'Corner running' for this: see Chapter 4), narrow their choice of Rights and Responsibilities to a maximum of 10.
- In groups the children choose either a Right or Responsibility. They then create a large image (it can be abstract) that represents to them what it means. This can be produced using art materials of their choice such as pastel, chalk, pencil, paint, collage etc. There should be a balance so that all the Rights and Responsibilities have been created visually.
- The final result should be covered in PVA glue to create a protective film (unless it is a collage) and then displayed around the classroom. The display stays there for the full academic year and is frequently referred to.

Suitable for

Any Key Stage

Variations

- The children create a personal folding book with an image for each Right and Responsibility. This is kept in their tray/desk or displayed on the wall in the classroom.
- The children create a video or animation of their class rules using *Digital Blue* technology (**www.digitalblue.org.uk**). The children would work in mixed-ability pairs (ensuring that the EAL pupil is placed with a confident and capable English speaker) and have one rule each. Once the rules have been created they can be played on a loop. It would be useful to have the video/animation playing on the smart board at the start of every day before the children arrive and whilst they are settling down.

Visual timetable

A visual timetable which is displayed is a useful guide for the child to feel secure and understand what is expected of them.

Aims

- To understand what happens and when in a school day
- To feel secure in the structure of a school day
- BIC

Vocabulary

Language related to subjects, e.g. Maths, Science, Physical Education
Language related to events, e.g. lunch, break, assembly, visitor
Language related to time, e.g. home time

Resources

- A large laminated daily timetable with times to break up the day
- Large images that relate to subjects, events and times that are placed on the timetable
- Velcro or Blu-Tack

What to do

- Create an A1 or larger daily timetable grid that has blank spaces and times for lessons and events. In the gaps on the grid include a Velcro strip or a piece of Blu-Tack. Make sure the grid is laminated so that it can be reused.
- Create large images that fit neatly into the empty squares of the timetable grid and place Velcro or Blu-Tack on the back of them. Make sure they are laminated so that they can be reused.

- Place the timetable at the front of the classroom and the large cards in an envelope next to it. Then stick the images in the spaces on the grid to show what will be happening and when it will be happening during the day. Once an event has happened, remove the image and place it in the envelope.

Suitable for

KS1, KS2

Variations

- Ask the EAL pupil to fill up the timetable at the start of the day and/or remove the images once the event has happened so that they are aware of what is happening when and where.
- Include words with the images so that the EAL pupil can read what the image means – eventually (as the year develops) use fewer of the visual images to show events and more of the words.
- The EAL pupil could make their own version using their home language.

Responsibility

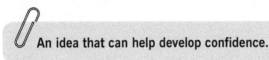

An idea that can help develop confidence.

Aims

- To understand the systems of the school/class
- To become a valued member of the class
- BIC

Vocabulary

Language related to responsibilities

Resources

- A rota with the children's names next to the activity

What to do

It's a good idea to give a responsibility to all of the children within a school year to foster self-esteem and confidence. An EAL pupil can be given the following responsibilities from the moment they arrive in the class even if they have limited English:

- Take the registers to the office
- Sharpen the pencils
- Clean the board
- Give out letters at the end of the day
- Tidy an area of the classroom

Suitable for

KS1, KS2

Variations

Eventually:

- Give out books/work that requires them to read because the work has names on it
- Remove an event from the timetable once it has happened
- Change the names on the class rota
- Be a class buddy
- Be a school council representative
- Take a message to a member of staff

'This is the way we . . .'

A fun class song that can encourage a pupil to use basic sentences that will be useful in class situations and help them to quickly understand how to do certain routines.

Aims

- To help the pupil understand some of the systems used within the school
- To develop vocabulary associated with routines
- BIC

Vocabulary

Days of the week
Months of the year
Language related to routines (see below)

Resources

None

What to do

This song is based on the tune 'Here We Go Round the Mulberry Bush!' (see Appendix 1: 'This is the way we . . .')

- You lead the song and encourage the children to keep singing until they have finished the action. For example, if you want the children to line up alphabetically for a fire alarm, sing softly and quietly 'This is the way that we stay safe for a school fire alarm' until all the children have lined up and are ready to leave safely and without noise.

'This is the way we . . .

. . . line up for lunch
. . . work quietly
. . . fold our arms
. . . leave the room
. . . line up from play
. . . sit ready for lessons
. . . get ready for home
. . . always stay safe (for a fire alarm test)
. . . start registration
. . . clean art pots
. . . give out the books
. . . tidy our desks
. . . dress for PE

(Sing the middle line three times)

. . . on a cold and frosty morning.
. . . on a warm and humid lunchtime.
. . . for a school fire alarm.
. . . for a quiet end to school time.'

Suitable for

KS1, KS2

Variations

- There are many ways to vary this idea. You could include sentences about the seasons, months of the year or days of the week, e.g. 'on a wet and windy Monday'; 'on a clear autumn morning'.

Chapter 4
Activities and ideas for verbal communication

Introduction

This chapter includes a selection of activities that encourage thinking skills and verbal communication. The intention is that the EAL pupil(s) will become more confident in speaking English if they have structured opportunities to practice, and so many of these ideas and activities are based on mixed-ability group work, talk partners and discussion.

Talk tokens

A simple idea that encourages reluctant speakers to speak more and pupils who take over an activity to speak less, thereby allowing everyone – no matter what their level of English – to communicate fairly.

Aims

- To provide a structured place for an EAL pupil(s) to practise English
- To communicate and listen as part of a mixed-ability group
- To take turns
- BIC/CALP

Vocabulary

Token
Spend
Phrases such as:
    I agree/disagree because . . .
    I think . . .
    I agree but perhaps . . .
    It is your turn to talk
    What do you think?
    Any ideas?
    I'm now listening

Resources

- A selection of discs that represent a token – you can make and laminate these, with the name 'talk token' emblazoned on each one. Every child in the class is given a set of 10 tokens for their personal use. They can be of any size, design and colour.

What to do

- At the start of any groupwork ensure that each child in the class has at least four talk tokens that they can 'spend' in the discussions.
- They can use their token to say one word, a sentence, an idea or a monologue. It is up to the child. Monitor and encourage all children to use their tokens and also remind them that once spent they can only contribute through listening and with non-verbal language such as nodding and 'hmm'.
- Encourage each child to use/spend all of their tokens by the end of the group discussion time. Once they have spent their token they have to listen and not interrupt others who still need to use their token.
- With confidence and time you will notice that the EAL pupil will speak more and for longer lengths of time. You will also notice that all children will be more considered in what they say and how they 'spend' their token.

Suitable for

Any Key Stage

Variations

- Ask the children to decide how many of their 10 talk tokens they want to spend in the discussion before it begins.
- The children make their own talk tokens.

Expert groups

This is a simple group activity that can be used in any subject and is great for gathering and remembering information. The aim is to learn something as a team and then pass this information on to others.

Aims

- To work as a team to research and learn facts about a given theme
- To teach/pass on information about a particular theme
- To gain confidence to talk within a group situation
- To gain an understanding of a particular class topic
- BIC/CALP

Vocabulary

Technical vocabulary associated with the subject matter, e.g. 2D or 3D shapes etc. Phrases such as:

Do you understand?
My theme is . . .
My 10 facts are . . .

Resources

- Worksheet for recording the information from the 'experts'
- Information books, the internet, DVDs etc. to support research into the theme
- 2D and 3D shapes to handle

What to do

- Place the pupils in mixed-ability groups of four and give each group a responsibility to find out information about a theme, for example the properties of a 2D or 3D shape. The groups are named A, B, C, D.

- Each group learns as much as they can about their theme so that they have a set of key facts that they can memorise. Every member of the group needs to become an 'expert'. The members of each group have to decide how they will remember their key facts so that they can eventually pass on their information to a new group.
- The children are rearranged so that each new group contains a member from group A, B, C and D. Each group therefore has at least one 'expert' for each theme, for example a 2D or 3D shape.
- The pupil from group A teaches what they know to their new group, i.e. they teach pupils from groups B, C and D about their shape. They can pass on their information in any way they choose but the rest of the group need to record this new information in some format. You may wish to provide the class with a worksheet/writing frame that will help them do this.
- By the end of the lesson each child will have become an 'expert' about one theme, for example a 2D or 3D shape, and gained general facts about the topic: for example, they will be an 'expert' about a cuboid while having a general understanding of 2D and 3D shapes.

Suitable for

Any Key Stage

Variations

- This activity can be used for a variety of subjects, such as looking at religious festivals so that a group becomes an expert about Judaism but gains a general understanding of celebration in Hinduism, Sikhism, Islam, Buddhism, Humanism and Christianity.
- If your EAL pupil has little understanding of English it would be advisable to pair them with a confident English speaker when they are placed in their second group so that they have support with their language.
- See 'Remember, remember' activity for an extension of this idea.
- See 'Talk tokens' as a method to help EAL pupils take part in the expert groups and limit some children taking over the research.

Remember, remember

This is a great Geography activity based on the well-known game of memorising objects under a cover.

Aims

- To encourage children to use geographical language
- To work as a team to recognise and memorise geographical features on a map
- To recreate a map
- BIC/CALP

Vocabulary

Places
Spaces
Continents
Oceans (names etc.)
Cities (names etc.)
Scale
Mountains (names etc.)
Longitude/latitude
Persuasive language:
    'No, it goes here because . . .'
    'It is south of Africa etc. . . .'
    'I've noticed that X is next to C because . . .'

Resources

- An outline of the map to be filled in with detail
- A large detailed map
- Various maps with different scales

What to do

- Place the pupils in mixed-ability groups of four. Show them the large map of the world, UK or a particular location such as their local area and explain that as a group they will take it in turns to come up and look at particular features (the map can be on a smart board and the slide-down feature can be used to hide and reveal it).
- Encourage them to look at major features such as oceans, continents, rivers, cities, landmarks etc. (depending on the map you are looking at).
- The children choose who will come to the board and look in detail at the map and what in particular they should look for. They then return to the tables and explain to their group what they found out and where it should go on their blank map.
- The aim is for them to remember as many features as possible and place them in the correct places on the map.

Suitable for

Any Key Stage

Variations

- Extend the activity to look at spaces and places (continents and oceans are considered spaces whereas cities and countries are places). Ask the children to give examples of which places are connected to other places by spaces, for example which countries are connected to other countries by oceans.

Snowball

This is a useful technique that helps to build confidence in speaking aloud and sharing ideas or opinions.

Aims

- To share ideas and information in groups of various sizes
- To develop confidence to share ideas
- To extend vocabulary through repeating language
- CALP

Vocabulary

Language associated with turn-taking
Language associated with listening
Language related to the topic they are discussing

Resources

- Possibly resource books for research
- Large piece of paper with coloured pens

What to do

- Group the pupils so that they are in mixed-ability pairs and give them a task that requires them to find facts and/or share ideas about a given topic: for example, find out about Henry VIII and his six wives.
- They then join up with another pair so that they become a group of four and share their ideas/information. They have to create a mind map or list that includes everyone's information/ideas.
- This group of four joins another four to make a group of eight and repeats the above.
- You could eventually snowball so that the whole class becomes one group that shares ideas, but usually it is best to stop at the group of four or eight, depending on what the activity is.

Suitable for

Any Key Stage

Variations

- The snowball activity can't really be adapted – however, the organisation of the groups can be. The children could be grouped with the eight children already on their tables or they could walk around the room to find pairings and groupings or they could be given specific children to work with that you have predetermined before the lesson.

Jigsaw

A technique that encourages pupils to develop language through fact finding and summarising and is great for a variety of curriculum areas.

Aims

- To develop teamwork
- To encourage the skills of summary and fact finding
- To share ideas and build confidence in speaking with a variety of pupils
- CALP

Vocabulary

Language associated with the theme, e.g. the Egyptians

Resources

- Work-cards, books, the internet, activity packs etc. for the expert group activities
- Large piece of paper and pens for the 'Home' group activity

What to do

- Place your pupils in mixed-ability groups of four and call each group a 'home' group.
- Ask each pupil in the group of four to find out information about a given theme, such as the Egyptians. For example, child A could focus on farming, child B look at religion and child C at making papyrus and how it is used. The children then regroup with others from different 'home' groups who are researching the same topic as themselves to form an 'expert' group (see 'Expert groups').
- The children in the 'expert' groups take part in an activity that enables them to learn about their topic and become 'experts'. They have to work as a team and gain as much information as possible. They record the information in some way.

- The children then return to their 'home' groups and start to pool their information. They each teach the rest of the group what they discovered about their topic and the 'home' group then produces some form of record such as a poster, flyer, or PowerPoint presentation about their theme.

Suitable for

KS2, KS3

Variations

- To start you would choose the home and expert groupings to ensure there is support for EAL learners in mixed-ability groups. However, over time you could allow the children to choose their own groups and how they wish to present their information.

Yeah, but . . .

This technique can be used in a variety of curriculum subjects. It is a good technique for structured debate and can help pupils form reasoned arguments.

Aims

- To form a reasoned opinion about a topic
- To conduct a debate and express opinion clearly
- To help a pupil refine what they think based on what others say
- To help a pupil refine what they think based on factual information (see Variation)
- CALP

Vocabulary

I think XXX because . . .
I can see what you mean but . . .
I disagree because . . .
I agree because . . .
Yeah, but . . .

Resources

- PowerPoint (see Variation)
- A large room

What to do

- Divide your class into two and ask the pupils to form two circles where one circle (A) is inside the other circle (B). The pupils in circle A face the pupils in circle B.
- Give the class a question or a topic to consider: for example, Should we hunt foxes? Should we always give aid to other countries?

- The pupil in circle A starts the discussion by stating what they think and why they have this opinion, then the pupil in circle B (who is standing/sitting opposite them) states what they believe to be true and why. They can have the same opinion but they may have a different reason for it.
- After a few minutes ask the pupils in circle B to move clockwise one space so that they are facing a new pupil in circle A. Circle A stays where they are.
- Pupil A starts the debate again and pupil B replies. This time, however, encourage the pupils to consider moderating their opinion based on what the previous child said.
- Continue to do this until you think the pupils have refined what they think and are able to express it to the best of their ability.
- Finally share opinions as a class.

Suitable for

KS2, KS3

Variations

- It is always best to have reasoned opinions in a debate but this can only happen if pupils have information to base their ideas on. It may be useful therefore to provide teachable moments throughout the discussion. To do this, create a selection of five slides or large posters that have facts on them about the topic that is being discussed and, after moving clockwise twice, show one of them to the class. Ask the pupils to try to consider the fact and, when they have the next person to debate with, encourage them to try to incorporate it into their reasoning.
- Pupil in circle A can be for the topic/question and B against it.
- Pupil in circle A can be of any opinion but pupil in circle B must have an opposite opinion.

Listen up!

This is a great role-play activity to help summarise information and recall facts. This technique can be used with a variety of curriculum subjects.

Aims

- To encourage listening skills
- To summarise information and use open-ended questions
- To develop the technique of story telling
- To be aware that listening isn't a passive activity
- CALP

Vocabulary

Who, where, what, when, why questions
Can you tell me . . .
   What happened next?
   Why do you think . . .?
   Where did it happen?
   When did it happen?
   Who was involved?
   How did you . . .?
I noticed . . .
I saw, heard, smelt
To summarise . . .

Resources

- Factsheet of information
- A prompt sheet for pupil B (not always necessary)
- A record sheet for pupil C (not always necessary)

What to do

- Place your pupils in mixed-ability groups of three and name them A, B, C.
- In role as a witness to something, pupil A has information to pass on or a story to tell to B and C. The information can be based on a historical event such as witnessing a Viking invasion, a fact sheet about a real life event, a class trip to a sacred space or something they have made up themselves.
- Pupil B is also in role and they are a reporter or police officer and have to glean all the information by asking questions, prompting pupil A and asking for clarification so as to find out as much as possible.
- Pupil C does not speak but does listen very carefully. They are permitted to make notes if they wish. Once A and B have completed their discussion, pupil C recalls what they heard and summarises the event/story/investigation.

Suitable for

KS2, KS3

Variations

- This does not have to be done in role. The pupils can be placed together so that they are simply storytelling or sharing opinions based on a scientific investigation. Pupil B would interview pupil A, who conducted the investigation with a different pupil.

Any questions?

This is a challenging but funny game that requires pupils to have a conversation purely through questions!

Aims

- To develop speaking and listening skills
- To develop verbal fluency and quick thinking
- To understand the various ways questions are used in the English language
- To consider the use of tone whilst speaking English
- CALP

Vocabulary

Vocabulary related to the topic
What, why, where, when, who, how

Resources

- You may wish to use flashcards or information cards about your theme, class topic, the lesson's focus (i.e. natural disasters) or information about current affairs.

What to do

- Group the pupils into threes and name them A, B and C. A and B will have the conversation and C will be the adjudicator.
- A starts the conversation with a question. B replies with another question. They need to keep the conversation going only through using questions. For example:

A = Have you seen the news today?
B = Why what's happened?
A = Haven't you heard about Haiti?
B = What about Haiti?
A = Could it have been an earthquake?
B = Didn't YOU say you saw the news?
A = Do you even know what an earthquake is?

- Pupil C, as the adjudicator, monitors the conversation and awards points. If a pupil makes a statement rather than a question, repeats a question or pauses too long then a point is awarded to the other pupil. Also if a question doesn't make sense then that pupil will lose a point. (Both start with zero points.)
- The game is over when the first pupil loses three points. At this point pupil C takes over the conversation and that pupil becomes the adjudicator.

Suitable for

KS2, KS3

Variations

- This idea can be adapted so it is a time-filler and two pupils are questioning at the front of the class while the rest watch.
- Use this technique as a plenary where the pupils have to review what they have learnt through questions. For example:

  A = What did you learn today?
  B = Didn't you pay attention?
  A = Don't you always see me work hard?
  B = Wasn't it about religious leaders?
  A = Do you know of one?
  B = Isn't the Pope the religious leader of the Roman Catholic church?
  A = What do you think?

The teacher's dog

This is a speaking game that can be adapted to suit different curriculum subjects and situations. It encourages quick thinking and the use of the alphabet and adjectives.

Aims

- To develop knowledge of adjectives and proper nouns
- BIC/CALP

Vocabulary

Adjectives
Proper nouns
The alphabet

Resources

- Possibly some dictionaries
- Possibly cards that have a visual representation of the adjectives

What to do

- This can be a class or a group activity and be used as a time-filler or as a starter to a lesson. The first pupil starts the game by saying the phrase, 'The teacher's dog is an XXX dog and his/her name is XXX'. They have to replace the XXX with a word beginning with the letter A (e.g. 'adventurous' and 'Arthur').
- The next pupil repeats the phrase but this time replaces XXX with a word beginning with the letter B.

- This is repeated with each child taking the next letter from the alphabet until they get to Z and then the game starts again but with a different animal and person. X can be 'ex', e.g. 'exceptional' etc. For example:

  Pupil 1 = The teacher's dog is an adventurous dog and his name is Arthur.
  Pupil 2 = No, the teacher's dog is a brilliant dog and his name is Brian.
  Pupil 3 = No, the teacher's dog is a cunning dog and her name is Chloe.
  Pupil 4 = No, the teacher's dog is a dopey dog and her name is Donna.

Suitable for

Any Key Stage

Variations

- This could be a written activity.
- The children could create their own version.
- Take part in the game using the home language of the EAL pupil(s) in the class.

Rainbow groups

A great technique to encourage children to work with a variety of people on a given task.

Aims

- To group EAL pupils so that they are able to learn with and from a variety of children in the class
- To develop team work
- BIC

Vocabulary

Vocabulary associated with the research
Language that is used for general group work such as . . .
    What shall I look up?
    Where can I find it?
    It's here!
    What shall I write down?

Resources

- The internet
- Resource books
- DVDs and CDs
- Questions that focus research
- Writing frame

What to do

- Each pupil is given a colour from the rainbow (red orange yellow green blue indigo violet) and then asked to join a group according to their colour, e.g. all reds together.
- They are asked to conduct a particular activity that they have to complete as a group.

- The outcome of each group's work is then pooled so that each colour makes a map of information about the topic.
- The final pieces of information are then used to write an informative piece using a writing frame as support.

Suitable for

Any Key Stage

Variations

- You can group the children in a variety of formats using colours: for example, all yellows and greens together, which could mean that groups are composed of children of the same or mixed abilities, or correspond to friendship groups.

Mime the job

This is a simple charades game that requires a pupil to mime a job and the rest of the class to guess what the job is.

Aims

- To think creatively and have some awareness of the various jobs available
- To develop confidence to mime in front of a group of peers
- BIC

Vocabulary

Titles for various jobs such as teacher, shopkeeper, dog walker, doctor, vet, nurse, bin-man/woman, lumber Jack/Jill, builder, games/software designer.

Resources

- Cards that list various jobs with a brief definition of what they are.

What to do

- Organise the class into mixed-ability groups of six. One pupil is chosen to conduct the mime. They take a card from the pack and then perform what it is, as simply as possible.
- The rest of the group try to guess what the job is. Whoever guesses correctly takes his/her turn to do a mime with a different card.

Suitable for

Any Key Stage

Variations

- To extend this idea ask the groups to try to categorise the jobs that they have in their cards. Then discuss how jobs can be categorised into specific employment structures, i.e. Primary, Secondary, Tertiary and Quaternary.
- You could do this as a class time-filler.
- Instead of miming jobs the pupils could mime school lessons, leisure time activities, sports, home chores such as cooking or washing up.

Story cloak

This activity involves the oral tradition of storytelling and asks the pupils to create a visual representation of it for a storytelling session.

Aims

- To be able to retell a familiar simple story
- To represent a story visually
- CALP

Vocabulary

Story
Retell
Cloak
Tradition
Sew
Paste/glue
Names of colours
Design
Bold
Language related to a story, such as suddenly, all at once, finally etc.

Resources

- Paper discs
- Coloured crayons, pens, ink or paint
- Pencils
- PVA glue
- Paper cape
- Willow pattern plate

What to do

- Place the pupils in mixed-ability groups of three. They have to remember a story that has been told to them (it can be a traditional story from the EAL pupil's home country or from the UK or a popular short story that they have read and enjoyed) and try to retell it in their own way. This can be through drama and re-enactment of the story.
- They then represent the story artistically on a large circular shape. They need to use simple shapes and bold colours to make it stand out from a distance (it can be painted or coloured with thick crayon and glued over with PVA glue to make it last). You could use a willow pattern plate as a stimulus.
- The discs from each group are then pasted onto a large paper cape. This cape is then worn by a child or adult during a story-telling time such as at the end of the day, during circle time or as a plenary.
- One of the discs displayed on the cloak is chosen. Whichever group created that disc becomes the storytellers for that session.

Suitable for

Any Key Stage

Variations

- The discs could be created as a sewing task and then transferred onto a cloth cloak as an appliqué and displayed in the classroom on a dressmaker's dummy.
- Look at 'Science – Language lab coat' for a similar idea!

Describing definitions

This game encourages defining a word, with the other pupils working out what it is.

Aims

- To improve knowledge of nouns
- To develop confidence to be able to describe and define a word
- To extend vocabulary lists
- BIC/CALP

Vocabulary

Nouns such as tree, car, dog, house, flower, carrot, bed, garage etc.
Nouns associated with a specific need of the EAL pupil(s) such as language related to family, school, food, shopping etc.

Resources

- List of words (some more difficult than others to define)

What to do

- Divide the pupils into mixed-ability groups of three or four and give them a letter, A, B, C, D
- A is given a list of words. Their task is to describe/define their word to B and C without saying the actual word. B and C have to work out what the word is. They have one minute per word.
- Pupil D is the adjudicator and has to monitor A, B and C, awarding points: one point for each correct word and none if they cheat
- Once all the words have been described a different child takes their turn to define a new set of words and another is the umpire.

Suitable for

Any Key Stage

Variations

- This can be a whole-class activity and be used as a time-filler or plenary activity where a child stands at the front of the class and defines a word. The whole class takes part and puts up their hands when they think they know the word. If correct then they define the next word etc.
- The list of nouns can be related to a specific curriculum subject, such as games in PE or musical instruments for Music, or related to the class topic.
- Turn the words into sentences or silly paragraphs.

Call My Bluff!

This was a popular TV game and is great for the classroom. It encourages creativity and quick thinking related to definitions of words.

Aims

- To extend vocabulary
- To develop confidence in using new and unfamiliar words in everyday situations
- CALP

Vocabulary

Words that describe and define

Resources

- Dictionaries
- Bilingual dictionaries
- White boards and pens

What to do

- Divide the class into mixed-ability groups of three. Each group has to use their dictionary to find an unusual word that they think the other groups would not know the meaning of. They then have to create three definitions for it. One definition is correct while the other two are false.
- The groups take turns to sit on the panel at the front of the class and read out their three definitions. They need to be as convincing as possible with all three. Good acting is required! For example:
  Word = Truculent
  Definition 1 = the name given to the journey an old truck
  Definition 2 = the word for when someone is argumentative or sullen
  Definition 3 = the word for when you give up treats at Lent

- The other groups have to work out which definition is the correct one and which are false. They then write the number of the definition they think to be correct (1, 2 or 3) on a white board and use the 'show me' technique to display it to you.
- The panel then say which definitions were wrong and what their word really means. If a group was correct with their guess work they win a point, if they were incorrect then a point is given to the team on the panel.
- This continues until all groups have taken a turn and all scores are added up. The team with the most points wins.

Suitable for

Any Key Stage

Variations

- This activity could be conducted with words and definitions from a bilingual dictionary and the home language of the EAL pupil(s) in your class.

Animate!

This idea should inspire groups to work creatively and produce a short animated movie.

Aims

- To create a movie that includes speech and movement
- To work and communicate in a team
- BIC/CALP

Vocabulary

Language associated with team work

Resources

- *Digital Blue Movie Creator* or Flip cameras (see below)
- Plasticine
- Paper
- Scissors
- Colouring items
- There are many resources on the digital market that are easy to use and include technology likely to be in school such as *Digital Blue Movie Creator* (http://www.digitalblue.org.uk) and Flip video cameras (http://www.theflip.com) which look more like phones and have a flip-out USB connection

What to do

- Use the digital recorders to film short animations of familiar stories, stories the children have created or news events (there are instructions on how to use the cameras online and with the packaging and it is useful to work out how to use them before teaching the skills to the children)
- Divide the children into small groups of three or four. Ensure that they are mixed ability and give the responsibility for the camera to the EAL pupil.

- Encourage the children to create a story board of a familiar story such as the Christmas story. Divide the scenes between the different groups.
- The groups now create a 3D version of the scene from the story using plasticine. Each part of the story board becomes a 3D frieze that will be filmed.
- Using a digital camera such as *Digital Blue Movie Maker*, the children take an image of each of the scenes and the characters. Whenever they move one of the characters they film it and save the image so that they begin to create a short animation of the scene.
- Once all animations have been created, edited and saved, put them in sequence and show the end result to the class.

Suitable for

KS2, KS3

Variations

- You can use other technology such as *Funny Faces* (**http://www.funnyfaces. com**) to create a caricature of a picture or *CrazyTalk* animation technology (**http://www.reallusion.com/crazytalk**) to animate an image.
- Flip Video can be used to film in real time and then edit, rather than making an animation.

Talk dolls

Talk dolls are also known as Persona dolls. They are similar to a rag doll but do not have a drawn face or clothes. Such dolls are fantastic for encouraging exploration of emotions and culture.

Aims

- To develop language related to emotional literacy
- To encourage empathy
- To create a forum where children do not feel inhibited about sharing feelings
- BIC/CALP

Vocabulary

Emotive language

Resources

- A selection of dolls

What to do

- Place your pupils in mixed-ability groups of three and give each group a doll and a thought/discussion card. Ask them to discuss the card and try to solve the dilemma, and in some cases create something. Such dilemmas could be:
  - This doll is an alien and has just landed from a planet you have never heard of. Create a suitcase with items inside which you think the alien will need for his/her first week at your school.
  - This doll has been abandoned. Why? How does he/she feel?
  - This doll has had to leave their home in a hurry. Draw/create the most important item they have brought with them and discuss how they feel about leaving.
  - This doll is worried. What could he/she be worried about?
  - How is this doll feeling today? Why?

- Once this has happened conduct a circle time session where the children speak through the doll about how they feel. Try to relate some of the issues to the children themselves.

Suitable for

KS1, KS2

Variations

- You could use the dolls to explore how the children feel about big questions such as death or anger etc. and the doll could be used to answer for the child.
- The answers and ideas that are developed in the discussions could be written in thought bubbles.
- Explore religious and cultural identity through the doll – e.g. What would a person wear to show that they belong? – and create clothes that show the doll's cultural identity.
- Re-enact familiar stories and events or celebrations using the dolls.

Repetition

This idea builds on the circle game activity of 'My granny went to market and bought . . .'.

Aims

- To develop memory and creativity
- To improve basic vocabulary and add to current knowledge
- To learn to use basic sentences and connectives
- BIC

Vocabulary

Any vocabulary related to shopping or whatever you feel the EAL pupil(s) needs to know
Basic sentences and connectives: and, so, but

Resources

- A ball or toy that is passed around to indicate turn-taking

What to do

Language that is repetitive is a useful aid for EAL learners because they can pick up certain words very quickly and begin to place them with others to develop new sentences.

- Sit in a circle and explain that they have to memorise a shopping list for Christmas. So the first pupil starts by saying
  This Christmas I asked Santa for . . . a doll.
  The second pupil says
  This Christmas Polly asked Santa for a doll but I asked for a car.
  The third pupil says
  This Christmas Rajeev asked Santa for a car and Polly asked for a doll but I asked for an iPod.
  The fourth pupil says
  This Christmas Lakshmi asked Santa for an iPod, Rajeev asked for a car and Polly asked for a doll but I asked for a dog.

- Carry on like this until they all have managed to create a shopping list and when you reach the final pupil all the class say the list aloud without the names and in order: doll, car, iPod, dog etc.

Suitable for

Any Key Stage

Variations

- The sentence and list can be any vocabulary that you think the EAL pupil(s) needs, for example:

    Actions – Yesterday I learnt how to jump . . .
    Routines in school – In school the teacher tells me to line up . . .
    Colours – My favourite colour is . . .
    Family – I have a brother who is funny . . . I have a sister who is naughty.
    Leisure – Last summer I went on holiday to Cornwall and it was hot.
    Descriptions – My teacher is unusual because he has green hair, my teacher is unusual because he has green hair and blue ears, my teacher is unusual because he has green hair, blue eyes and is an alien (this teacher could be drawn after the circle time!).

- You could also link these lists and sentences to actions and/or visual images so that the pupils understand what the word means and aren't simply saying it without context.

Corner running

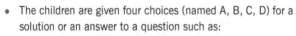

The children consider what they think about something and then make a choice out of four options. This method can also be used for assessment.

Aims

- To develop opinion
- To communicate opinion in a pair
- To begin to understand democracy
- BIC/CALP

Vocabulary

Choose
Corner
Run/walk

Resources

- Labels for the corners
- Good idea to do this in the hall or playground so that they can run

What to do

- The children are given four choices (named A, B, C, D) for a solution or an answer to a question such as:
  'Should animals be experimented upon?'
  A: Yes, definitely for everything.
  B: Yes, but only for medicines.
  C: No, definitely not for anything.
  D: Not sure.
  The labels for the choices are placed in the four corners of the room or on four different tables.

- In mixed-ability pairs the children decide which option they agree with and then when you say 'now choose' they walk/run to their choice.
- The numbers are added up and narrowed to two options and the children choose again.
- The class make their final choice so that they come to a conclusion.

Suitable for

Any Key Stage

Variations

- A part-time trainee called Chris did 'Corner running' as part of the plenary of a Geography lesson. The children had to decide where various animals came from. Each option was a different continent and reinforced the learning that had happened in the lesson.
- You may use this method for more complicated issues such as researching a particular question about a topic or deciding as a class what part of a topic you wish to study first, second etc. As you are all unsure which is the most important one to focus on first, corner running can help you decide in a democratic way.

Circle time

Circle time is a popular activity in most schools and has become a useful tool for PSHCE through the SEAL project. It is a great activity to help develop confidence in speaking and encourage active listening.

Aims

- To develop confidence in speaking and justifying personal opinion
- To use language to describe feelings
- To encourage speaking in a group and taking part in active listening
- BIC/CALP

Vocabulary

Repetitive sentences
Rules
Language associated with emotions
Language associated with opinion and reasoning

Resources

- Object to hold whilst speaking such as a soft toy or squashy ball

What to do

- Decide on a topic to focus on before you start and then begin the circle time session by sitting the class in a circle and explaining the rules of circle time, which are:

  1. You can only speak when you are holding the circle time object.
  2. You must listen and not interrupt anyone.
  3. You should not laugh at anybody's opinions and ideas.
  4. Circle time is a safe place to talk about feelings and so things should not be repeated or ridiculed. We should all show respect to each other.

- Start the discussion with a sentence related to the focus that will be repeated by each child, such as:

  - I think . . .
  - I believe . . . because . . .
  - My favourite thing is . . . because . . .
  - I would never . . . because . . .
  - I disagree/agree because . . .
  - The image makes me feel . . .
  - Today I feel . . . because . . .

- Encourage the children to respond to what each of the others say and so take part in active listening. Circle time will become a forum for discussing relevant issues and stating personal opinion. It can also be a place to express emotion and feelings.
- End the session by stating that everything during circle time is for sharing and so should be respected, then thank them for sharing.

Suitable for

Any Key Stage

Variations

- Provide a box in the classroom with pieces of paper and pens nearby. The pupils can anonymously write problems, concerns or issues on the paper and place them in the box. The box is then emptied during circle time and the children discuss how to solve the problem.
- Use poetry or an image, advert or painting as a stimulus for the discussion. A good book with lots of ideas for circle time is Gutteridge and Smith, 2008 (see Further Reading).

Record my story

> This activity requires the pupils to write a story and make it come alive through recording it.

Aims

- To work as a team to create an interesting descriptive story
- To learn to read a story with various inflections in the voice
- BIC/CALP

Vocabulary

Story
Beginning, middle, end
Conflict
Resolution
Recording
Expression
Low, high, loud, soft, quiet sounds
Whisper, shout
Speech
Character

Resources

- Digital recorder
- PC
- Paper and pens

What to do

- In mixed-ability groups of three, ask the children to write, redraft and complete a story. It must have a beginning, middle and end. It must contain approximately three characters, descriptive language and speech.
- Once they have created their story they need to decide how to divide it up so that it can be recorded. They need to choose who will read what and how it is to be read aloud.
- The groups practise reading the story aloud to each other and then to other groups, gaining feedback on how to improve the performance. They will practice how to change their voice for different characters, how to sound (e.g.) surprised and develop expression when reading aloud.
- Finally they record their story using a digital recorder and save it onto a CD.
- Ask the pupils to create a front cover for their CD and then place it in the class or school library.

Suitable for

Any Key Stage

Variations

- One of the stories could be performed and recorded by the whole class.
- The story could be retold using puppets and then filmed.

Mystery

This activity idea requires the pupils to work together to find a solution to a problem. It involves discussion, reasoning and analysis to decide on an answer.

Aims

- To develop thinking and problem-solving skills
- To work as a team
- To develop the skills of reasoning
- To learn to categorise information
- CALP

Vocabulary

Reasoning language such as:
    I think XXX because . . .
    I agree/disagree with this statement because . . .
    That is/is not relevant because . . .
    The answer is XXX because . . .
    Let's sort it . . .

Resources

- Twenty statements on laminated cards for each group
- A problem question displayed prominently in the classroom
- A piece of A1-sized sugar paper for each group that will be their 'tablecloth of relevance'

What to do

- Place the pupils in mixed-ability groups of three and put a piece of A1 sugar paper, which will act as their 'tablecloth of relevance', in the middle.
- Now give them a problem/question to solve. Explain that they have to work together to read the cards which have clues on them to work out what the solution may be. They have to justify their answers with relation to the cards.
- Provide each group with a set of cards (see below for an example) with various statements on them.
- Instruct the groups to lay the cards on the table and read the statements to each other.
- The groups place in the centre of their 'tablecloth of relevance' any statements they think are relevant to the question. If a statement isn't relevant they place it outside the tablecloth and if they think it might be relevant but are not sure at this stage then they place it on the edge.
- Once they have sorted and categorised the cards into **Relevant, Not relevant, Might be relevant** they re-read the **Relevant** section and try to put the cards in order of significance, i.e. from the most likely reason to the least likely reason.
- The pupils then look over the **Might be relevant** section and see if these cards are still relevant or if they can reject them.
- Finally they try to decide on the likely answer to the question/problem. They decide how to answer the question/problem and which cards show the strongest evidence. You may wish for them to write a paragraph that they will read aloud to the class at the end of the session. It is important to note that there may be more than one likely answer to the question. If it can be supported with evidence from the statement then more than one answer is fine. It is important to stress that it is the process rather than the outcome that is important in this activity.

Example

Mrs J. Wilson likes to go on holiday every year. Where did she go this year and why?

This question can be extended to discuss 'What sort of holiday has she had this year?'

She does not like to fly because she has a fear of flying	She has been to France, Canada, America, Germany, Spain and Russia	She likes to go on holiday with her children and grandchildren	She has not got a lot of money because she is a pensioner	She doesn't mind any type of weather but doesn't like it too hot
She went on holiday to Cornwall, Hampshire and Scotland when she was a Brownie and a Guide	She likes to travel by train and car	She enjoys seaside holidays	She has not travelled around the UK since she was a child	She cannot drive
She enjoys relaxing holidays with some sight-seeing	She lives alone	She likes to ride bicycles	She went on a cruise last year	Holidays in the UK are more popular since the 'credit crunch'
She gets sick on coaches	Holidays abroad are getting more expensive	When she was a child she would go camping in Wales with her family and has lots of fond memories	She has a dog	She has a motorhome

There are a few solutions to the question but the main one would be that she has been camping in her motorhome because she doesn't have a lot of money, and she went with her grandchildren. Her children drove. She would probably holiday in Wales, because she has fond memories of it, or somewhere else in the UK rather than abroad, because of the weather, the cost of travel and because she has not seen much of the UK.

Suitable for

KS2, KS3

Variations

- You can take this concept and make it more subject-specific so that the pupils learn about certain facts or analyse key information. A good book to explore this concept is Leat and Nichols, 1999 (see Further Reading).
- There are some good websites that include mysteries, thinking skills and problem solving:
  http://kids.mysterynet.com
  http://42explore.com/mystery.htm

Sing to remember!

This activity idea is useful to help embed key facts and access learning because it involves singing repetitive sentences.

Aims

- To use repetitive language to learn specific facts or events
- To use song and music to help learn a class topic
- CALP

Vocabulary

Vocabulary related to the class topic

Resources

- Paper and pens for creating the pupils' own versions of the song
- Key facts that you want incorporated into the song displayed in some way to the pupils

What to do

- In mixed-ability groups of three the pupils create their own version of a familiar song by changing the lyrics. They use key language and facts related to the class topic to create actions that complement each line of the song. Provide them with information that you want them to incorporate into their song in some way.
- They then share their version with the class and teach them how to sing it and mime the actions.
- See Appendix (p. 258) for example with the tune of a familiar song such as 'One Finger One Thumb Keep Moving'.

Suitable for

KS1, KS2

Variations

- This can be used as a way to start a class topic to showcase what they will find out, or equally at the end of one as a way to consolidate what they have learnt.
- This idea can be used with any familiar song that has simple repetitive language, for any curriculum subject.

Chapter 5
Activities and ideas for written communication

Introduction

This chapter has lots of activities that stimulate reading and writing. The activities can be adapted for any Key Stage and encourage confidence in writing English through modelling, scaffolded approaches to teaching and repetition. The ideas encourage 'talking for writing' techniques.

The pen is mine!

Often when you place pupils in groups there is a dominant child who monopolises the discussion and task. On such occasions the EAL pupil(s) can be left doing nothing and not learning. This simple idea enables the EAL pupil(s) to have a full role in the activity.

Aims

- For all pupils to take part in a group activity
- To help EAL pupils write English
- BIC

Vocabulary

The alphabet
General phonemes
Language related to sharing such as:
    Write this down
    Your turn
    You spell it like . . .
    Put it here
    Shall we use a different colour?

Resources

- Large piece of paper and pens
- Bilingual dictionary

What to do

- Divide pupils into mixed-ability groups of three. Name them A, B, C (B is the EAL pupil).
- Place the EAL pupil between the two other pupils and give them the responsibility of the pen and state that the only person who is allowed to write is pupil B.
- Pupils A and C discuss with B what to write and are allowed to help B with spelling etc.

Suitable for

Any Key Stage

Variations

- It is not only the pen that the pupil can be responsible for. They can also be the person who holds cards, paper, other resources etc.

Words and pictures

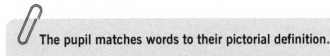

The pupil matches words to their pictorial definition.

Aims

- To develop vocabulary of high-frequency words
- BIC/CALP

Vocabulary

High-frequency words
Words related to the class topic or theme

Resources

- Laminated word and picture cards (A5 for KS1, smaller for KS2)
- Bilingual dictionary

What to do

- Provide the EAL pupil with a selection of pictures and words. They have to match the correct image with the correct picture, such as school, dog, pencil etc.
- To make this more fun and interesting it is useful to turn the cards into a game with another pupil (not EAL) where they have all images and words face-down and the children take it in turns to turn over two cards, trying to match a word and a picture. If correct they keep the pair, if incorrect they place it back down. The child with the most pairs wins. This activity is also known as *Pelmanism*.
- To reinforce the words, at the end of the activity it is always worth discussing the images and words with the EAL pupil and asking for the translation in their home language or chatting about how that word can become a sentence.

Suitable for

KS1, KS2

Variations

- The cards could be dual language cards.
- Eventually the written definitions of the words can be included with the images.
- You could encourage putting some of the words into silly sentences.

Hunt the fish!

This activity is a word game for mixed-ability pairs or groups of four. The children have to try to find matching fish by reading flashcards.

Aims

- To develop sight recognition of high-frequency words
- To improve vocabulary
- To encourage teamwork
- BIC/CALP

Vocabulary

High-frequency words
'I think my fish is behind the card that says . . .'

Resources

- Coloured fish
- Fish holders
- Word flashcards
- A4-sized coloured cards

What to do

- Randomly put the fish in the holders so that the coloured heads cannot be seen. Include a flashcard in front of each fish.
- Each pupil is then given an A4-sized card with six spaces for fish. The cards are different colours and correspond with the colours of the fish.
- The pupils take it in turn to say the sentence 'I think my fish is behind the card that says XXX'. They replace XXX with the word on the flashcard. They then look at the fish that is behind that

flashcard. If it is the same colour as their card they take the fish and place it on one of the spaces. If it isn't the same colour they replace it and it is the next pupil's turn to choose a flashcard.
- The aim is to fill their card with fish of the same colour.

This game can be purchased, but it can be made quite easily.

Suitable for

KS1, KS2, KS3 – choose words that are relevant to stages of development and age.

Variations

- This activity can be adapted by changing the words on the flashcards. Relate them to a class topic or a specific vocabulary list the EAL pupil needs.
- Change the flashcards so that they are sentence starters and the pupils have to create sentences.

Jigsaw a letter

A simple activity that enables children to self-correct and learn the structure of a letter by jigsawing pieces together.

Aims

- To help children understand the structure of a formal and informal letter
- BIC/CALP

Vocabulary

Construct, deconstruct, reconstruct
Letter
Address
Signed: From, love, yours faithfully, yours sincerely
Business
Informal/formal letter
Envelope
Dear . . .
Date

Resources

- A laminated letter written on a large piece of paper such as A3 that has been cut into jigsaw pieces

What to do

- At the start of an English lesson teach all children the structure of a letter through large visual aids and discussion. Try to provide visual examples and modelling.
- As part of the task, in the middle of the lesson give the jigsaw to the EAL pupil. Either in a mixed-ability pair or individually, they try to reconstruct the letter through trial and error.
- At the end of the lesson place the EAL pupil with a talk partner and ask each child to explain visually and verbally the structure of a letter.

Suitable for

KS1, KS2 – adapt to suit the needs and age of the class.

Variations

- This could be created using Smart Board technology, with the children reconstructing the letter by moving the electronic pieces, either as a class or individually.
- Cut the jigsaw into smaller pieces to make it more difficult.
- This activity can also be used for rhyming poetry. The children reconstruct the poem line by line.

Writing frames

A writing frame is a simple scaffold that supports children with writing and can slowly be removed so that they write independently. It can be used for any genre of writing.

Aims

- To develop confidence in writing independently
- To develop abstract vocabulary
- BIC/CALP

Vocabulary

Writing frame
Vocabulary
Sentence
Connective

Resources

- A selection of large laminated writing frames that vary in difficulty
- A selection of white board markers

What to do

- A writing frame is similar to a worksheet with a selection of sentence starters and connectives that help the writer consider what to write. The writing frame helps the writer structure their writing. Many can be purchased from publishers and the internet; however, it is simple to create your own so that it matches a specific text that you are looking at in class. It is essential that you explain in advance how to use it, and discuss the content.
- Provide your EAL pupil(s) with a selection of vocabulary that they can use with the frame and which have pictorial definitions next to them.

- In a mixed-ability pair the EAL pupil uses white board markers to write on the laminated frame, completing each sentence. They are encouraged to see this writing as a draft, and so changing their work is a positive experience.
- During the lesson check that they are aware of how to use a frame and that it is pitched at the correct cognitive and vocabulary level for them.
- See Appendix 2 for examples.

Suitable for

Any Key Stage, although writing frames are usually suitable for EAL pupils who have some level of understanding of the structure of sentences and so are likely to be at stage 2 or above in their development (see Chapter 1).

Variations

- There are many good websites for writing frames:
  http://www.sparklebox.co.uk/cll/writing/frames/
  http://www.skillsforlifenetwork.com/?atk=917
  http://www.primaryresources.co.uk/english/englishC1d.htm

Sequencing a story

The pupils have to use a variety of cues to support their understanding of the sequence of the story, which has been muddled up. They put the pages into the correct order.

Aims

- To use a variety of 'searchlight' cues to help decipher the sequence of a story
- To read a story and be able to retell it
- BIC/CALP

Vocabulary

Page
Book
Sequence
Order
A4 binder
Picture
Illustration

Resources

- An A4 ring binder
- Laminated pages from a text, with holes punched in them

What to do

- Remove the binding from a picture book, laminate each page and punch holes where the spine would be. Make sure that the pages are not numbered.
- Give the mixed-up pages to the EAL pupil(s), who have to read the text, look at the illustrations and try to put them back in their original order. They clip the pages into the A4 ring binder in the order they think is correct.

- They then have to explain verbally to you why they chose the pages in the order that they did and what is happening in the story. If they are incorrect let them try again but do not tell them which pages are in the wrong place. They will need to see if their order makes sense.

Suitable for

KS1

Variations

- This activity can be with a big book or a small book. To make it more challenging you could have two similar books that have been muddled and need reconstructing.

Sentence starters

A simple activity that involves reconstructing sentences that have been jumbled up.

Aims

- To understand the structure of an English sentence
- To understand how certain words make meaning when put together
- CALP

Vocabulary

Sentence
Capital letter
Full stop
Start
End
Connective
Jigsaw

Resources

- A selection of sentences that have been cut into two or more pieces and laminated.

What to do

- Have a selection of sentences cut into two or three pieces. The pieces can be cut so that they match exactly (like a jigsaw) or can have the same join, so that every start of a sentence could match with any of the endings, making the task more difficult.
- The pupil matches the pieces together to create sentences that make sense. Ask them to read the sentences to you and explain what they mean. It is always useful to make the sentences about the class topic so that they are relevant and/or about something the child is interested in.

Suitable for

Any Key Stage. The sentences can be as complex as the capabilities of the pupil and so can include connectives, punctuation, subordinate clauses etc.

Variations

- This activity can be conducted individually or in mixed-ability pairs.
- The children have to match the sentence starters and ends and then make a silly story or paragraph from them.

The writing is on the wall

A quick interactive and visual way to discover children's opinions. It requires them to write or draw their responses to a theme displayed on a wall or on a large piece of paper.

Aims

- To share personal opinions and reflections in a non-threatening environment
- BIC/CALP

Vocabulary

Language associated with reasoning

Resources

- Large sheet or large piece of paper (e.g. the back of wallpaper, which some hardware stores will donate as part of their community links)
- Different coloured pens or paint

What to do

- At the start of the day display the sheet and explain to the class that it is for them to write or draw their opinion and reflection on. Remind the children that spelling is not important for this activity.
- Provide them with a starting sentence based on their class theme or PSHCE topic, such as:
    - I think bullying is . . .
    - War is . . .
    - School is . . .
    - I believe . . .
    - I feel . . .
    - I want to know . ..
    - Why . . .

- Throughout the day the children take various opportunities to write or draw their reflections, thoughts, opinions etc. on the wall either individually or as a group. You need to remind them that each child should take the opportunity to write/draw their reflection. If necessary use talk tokens (see Chapter 2).
- At the end of the day share the responses with the class and discuss the various opinions displayed. It is essential that the opinions are anonymous.

Suitable for

KS2 and KS3; can be adapted for KS1

Variations

- This idea could be used at the start of a topic/theme/subject to collate what the children know and what they would like to find out. It could be similar to a thought shower and be used as a guide for planning.
- This could be a group activity where each mixed-ability table is given a sheet to write/draw on and then all the pieces are sewn or glued together to make one large sheet similar to a patchwork quilt.
- Instead of a sheet of paper you could use white board pens and the class window or tablecloth.

Question bombing!

A fun activity that creates class questions and is good for collating ideas at the start of a topic.

Aims

- To be able to create a question based on interest
- To write a basic question
- To read a question and sentence
- BIC/CALP

Vocabulary

Language related to the theme
What, where, why, when, how, who
Question mark

Resources

- Paper
- Pens

What to do

- Provide each mixed-ability pair with a piece of paper.
- Each pair writes a question on the paper related to what they want to find out about a theme, issue or class topic.
- Once the question is written the pair screw the paper into a ball and find someone across the room they want to throw it to.
- After the count of three the children throw their paper bomb (shouting – if you wish – GERONIMO!) to the person they identified. They then pick up the bomb that was thrown at them.
- They open their new bomb and read the question to themselves.
- After the chaos has calmed down and each child knows what their new question is, they take it in turn to read aloud and either you or the class answer each one.

Suitable for

Any Key Stage

Variations

- Instead of a bomb the children could make a paper plane and throw that.
- Instead of paired work, each child, if able, could create their own question.
- This could be a good starter for a PSHCE circle time session.

Moving mobiles

A simple activity that is a word bank of common words and phrases.

Aims

- To develop vocabulary lists
- To read and recognise high-frequency words and phrases
- BIC/CALP

Vocabulary

Adjectives
Basic sentences
Pronouns
Common connectives: and, but, then
Verbs

Resources

- Paint
- Card
- Wire hangers
- Glue
- Crayons
- Pencils

What to do

- In mixed-ability groups of three the children are given a selection of common phrases and high-frequency words that they use in their writing or come across in their reading.
- They write them out with images (it is essential they have images to support understanding) that show what they mean on large paper with colourful paint or thickly coloured crayon. The images and words/phrases are then either laminated or covered in PVA glue to make them stiff.

- The words and phrases are cut out and sewn or glued onto wire hangers or stiff card to make mobiles.
- The mobiles are hung in the classroom and referred to frequently when writing or reading.

Suitable for

KS1, KS2

Variations

- The words could be related to the class theme or topic or particular literacy targets such as interesting adjectives etc.

Sentence matching

A matching game where the pupils match sentence starters to sentence endings.

Aims

- To develop understanding of sentence structure
- CALP

Vocabulary

Any sentences that relate to the class topic or subject

Resources

- Laminated cards

What to do

- The EAL pupil(s) can do this activity alone or with a partner.
- The pupil has a set of cards that have starters and endings. They have to place them on the table face up and then match the sentence starter to an ending that makes sense or is silly. The sentence ending can match more than one sentence starter.
- The pupil makes sentences about their class topic or something related to their interest such as their home town.

Suitable for

Any Key Stage

Variations

- Once they have connected the sentences the pupils make a paragraph with a friend.
- It might be useful to include an image with each sentence that visually summarises the sentence or to ask the pupil to do this.

Mix and match!

A fun activity based on books that mix and match images and words such as *Ketchup on Your Cornflakes?* by Nick Sharratt and *Maisy's Mix and Match Mousewear* by Lucy Collins (see Further Reading).

Aims

- To create their own mix and match book
- To develop vocabulary
- BIC/CALP

Vocabulary

Language related to the theme of the book

Resources

- Card
- Colouring pens/pencils
- Pencil
- ICT word program (if you wish to make the books electronically rather than by hand)

What to do

- Show the mix and match books to the class and discuss how, by flipping one part of the book, you can make a silly sentence/question.
- In mixed-ability twos or threes the children decide what their book's theme will be. They can create a book which has 12 sentences that can be repeated and mixed up, e.g. Do you wear shoes on your feet? Do you wear knickers on your bottom? Do you wear gloves on your hands? etc. This then becomes a flip book that mixes up the clothes and body part words
- The children laminate each section so it is robust and then connect it to the spine using spiral binding.
- The book is shared with the rest of the class and placed in the class library.

Suitable for

Any Key Stage

Variations

- This can be created using the PC rather than by hand.
- The book could be dual language.

Label the classroom

Celebrating diversity by each EAL pupil creating dual-language labels for items in the class.

Aims

- To choose what to label and have fun taking ownership of their learning space
- To develop vocabulary lists
- BIC

Vocabulary

Names of furniture
People's names
Basic sentence structure
Basic language such as 'How do I spell . . .?'

Resources

- Card
- Coloured pencils/pens
- Laminator and laminates or sticky-back plastic
- Bilingual dictionaries – if not possible then children's English dictionaries
- Blu-Tack

What to do

- Provide a bank of cards at the side of the class and a variety of coloured pens.
- Whenever an EAL pupil has completed some work and has 'down' time, they take up a pen of their favourite colour (ideally a different colour per child) and then make a dual-language label (with pictures) for something in the class. It can even be you!
- They then laminate the card (or use sticky-back plastic) and stick it on the item they are labelling.

If there is more than one language in the class then eventually the class will be covered in a variety of languages as a celebration of the diverse languages and cultures in your school.

Suitable for

Any Key Stage

Variations

- This can be developed into sentences such as 'I am the teacher and my name is . . .'; 'This is the door and it is blue'.

Venn diagram

This idea helps organise ideas and promotes discussion.

Aims

- To categorise and discuss statements about a given topic
- To use thinking skills and to justify opinion
- CALP

Vocabulary

Language related to the subject being taught
Basic sentences

Resources

- A Venn diagram on A3 paper
- A set of statements on cards

What to do

- The children are in mixed-ability threes and are provided with a large Venn diagram and a set of cards that need to be sorted.
- They have to read each card and discuss which category it definitely belongs to and which it shares with others.

  For example: the theme is for a Religious Education lesson on religious practice. The children have cards that they have to put under what a Christian or Muslim may do:
  - They pray every day
  - They go on pilgrimage
  - They have festivals as part of worship
  - They worship Allah
  - They worship Jesus Christ
  - They pray to saints
  - They believe in angels
  - They cover their heads as a mark of respect

Muslim   Christian

- Once they have categorised the cards, they discuss the areas that are similar, as a class.

Suitable for

KS2, KS3

Variations

- This could be extended into a written piece through using a writing frame about similarities and differences etc.

What's my word?

The children take it in turns to work out what a mystery word is by listening to how many letters it has and how many letters it shares with another word.

Aims

- To use logical thinking strategies
- CALP

Vocabulary

Any word that is related to what the EAL pupil needs to know or to the class topic or subject.

Resources

- A set of cards with a basic word written on them, each with a corresponding image
- Dictionary

What to do

- Place the children in mixed-ability groups of three or four. Give them a set of cards that no one is allowed to look at. They are face down in the centre of the table.
- The first child takes the top card and without showing the others finds out what it means (if they are not sure) and says 'My word has XX letters, what do you think it is?' They take it in turns to guess the word. For example:

  Child A: My word has three letters, what do you think it is?
  Child B: Dog.
  Child A: My word shares one letter with dog.
  Child C: Hog.
  Child A: My word shares two letters with Hog.

Child D: Log.
Child A: My word shares one letter with Log.
Child B: Ahh! HOT!
Child A: Yes, my word is Hot.

- Once they have discovered the word, it is the next child's turn.

Suitable for

KS1, KS2

Variations

- Do this activity with paper to help, or in teams of two within the group rather than individually.
- Use longer words, or different rules rather than how many letters.

Letter ladders

How many words can they make using a route word or letter?

Aims

- To begin to see how words are similar
- To develop spelling strategies
- CALP

Vocabulary

Any

Resources

- Dictionary

What to do

- Place your pupils in mixed-ability pairs or threes (eventually the EAL pupil can work alone) and give them a route word/letter such as **a**, **i**, **be**.
- The group has to create a list of words that derive from this route. For example:

    ab
    Able
    Table
    Tablet
    Tab-letter
- The aim is for the pair to make as long a ladder as possible.

Suitable for

KS2

Variations

- Instead of creating a ladder from the smallest to the longest, you could create it from a long word to the smallest.

Word finder

How many words can you find in another? A good time-filler and starter.

Aims

- To recognise familiar words
- To develop vocabulary of unfamiliar words
- BIC/CALP

Vocabulary

Any

Resources

- Pens, paper
- List of words
- Dictionaries

What to do

- Provide the class with a very long word.
- Place the pupils in mixed-ability pairs. Together they aim to find as many words as possible hidden within that word.
- The pair with the most words wins.

Suitable for

KS1, KS2

Variations

None

Discussing drama to help writing

Miming or acting out a story can help a child realise what makes sense and what doesn't in terms of plot etc. This idea builds on how drama is a starter for writing.

Aims

- To use drama to help reinforce creative writing
- To work as part of a team
- To develop the use of descriptive language for writing with the aid of a friend
- BIC/CALP

Vocabulary

Adjectives
Plot
Character
Creative writing

Resources

- Large piece of paper and pens for thought shower
- Props for drama such as clothing or hats etc.
- White boards for shared writing activities
- White board pens

What to do

- To enable the children to write a story ask them to work in groups of mixed-ability threes or fours to act out their story-plot.
- Once they have acted it, ask them to create a story map of their plot and then a selection of thought showers that include:
    - how each character was feeling
    - descriptive words related to what the characters look like
    - descriptive words and sentences about the atmosphere at different parts of the plot

- Over time, the group collectively write the different parts of the plot, including some of the ideas they gained from the drama and discussion.

Suitable for

Any Key Stage

Variations

- The group can be divided so that a pair writes one part of the plot, the other pair writes another part and then they collectively redraft to make the parts work together as one story.
- Use props such as clothing (hats, scarves, gloves and bags) or create laminated character cards which the children use to become that character and act like them as a preparation to writing.

Adjective, noun, verb

A matching game where the pupils match sentence starters to sentence endings.

Aims

- To know what an adjective, noun or verb is
- To begin to understand basic sentence structure
- BIC

Vocabulary

List of adjectives
List of common nouns
List of verbs

Resources

- Paper
- Dictionary
- Pencils

What to do

- In mixed-ability groups of four, each child has a long piece of paper.
- They have to think of an adjective and write it on the top of the paper. They fold the paper down so no one can see the word and then pass the paper to the child on their right.
- Next, they write a noun (on the paper that has just been handed to them) and fold the paper down, passing it to their right.
- Next, they write a verb and fold the paper down and pass it to their right.
- Finally they open up the paper and try to make a sentence using the three words.

Suitable for

Any Key Stage

Variations

- This can be extended so that the group makes a paragraph from all four sentences.
- They can develop this to include more adjectives or adverbs etc.

Kung Fu punctuation

A fun, kinaesthetic method of recognising and using punctuation which is based on Ros Wilson's work.

Aims

- To recognise punctuation and understand how it is used
- To develop the use of punctuation
- CALP

Vocabulary

Brackets
Full stop
Comma
Question mark
Exclamation mark
Colon
Semicolon
Speech marks

Resources

None, although it is fun to have a prop such as a karate belt for each child

What to do

- Explain to the class that you will be reading a text together but that every time they come across grammar such as punctuation, they have to do a karate move. There are specific movements related to each form of punctuation. For example:
    - When they come to a full stop they punch the air in front of them and shout FULL STOP!

- When they come to a question mark they make the shape in the air for the top of the mark (at the same time shouting QUESTION!) and for the stop at the bottom of the mark they punch and shout MARK!
- When they see an exclamation mark they cut the air vertically in a downwards motion and shout EXCLAMATION! and then for the stop at the bottom they make a punch and shout MARK!

• For more information on Kung Fu punctuation watch
Youtube example: http://www.youtube.com/watch?v=U4sHIFmvg5c
Teachers' TV example: http://www.teachers.tv/videos/ks1-ks2-english-the-multilingual-classroom (there are links to this video that are also useful for EAL)
TES resources: http://www.tes.co.uk/teaching-resource/Kung-Fu-Punctuation-6061700/

Suitable for

KS3, KS2 but can be adapted for KS1

Variations

There are quite a few resources that support grammar in a fun way on the internet. Take a look at Bitesize on the BBC:
http://www.bbc.co.uk/schools/ks1bitesize/literacy/
http://www.bbc.co.uk/schools/ks2bitesize/english/spelling_grammar/

Chapter 6
Activities and ideas for visual aids and interactive teaching

Introduction

As discussed in Chapter 1, visual aids and interactive teaching techniques
are essential methods of supporting EAL learners because they visually and
physically interpret what can otherwise be difficult to comprehend. An EAL child
is more likely to develop CALP skills if they are involved in discussion alongside
kinaesthetic and visual learning. The activities in this chapter build on this premise
and provide you with ideas on how to improve learning in a variety of subjects.

English - Buzz off!

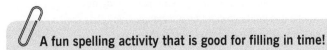

A fun spelling activity that is good for filling in time!

Aims

- To be able to spell simple words
- CALP

Vocabulary

Any vocabulary list that needs to be learnt, such as high-frequency words or
words associated with a topic
General words an EAL pupil needs to know
Words that have similar letter blends

Resources

- Lists of words that you wish to spell
- A set of cards for each word (this may not always be necessary)

What to do

- The children stand behind their seats.
- Explain the order that you will go around the class and then read aloud
  a word that is to be spelled.
- Each child in order will say the letter of that word. For example: You
  say 'The word to be spelled is DOG' and you hold up a card with a
  visual image of that word:
  - Child 1 – D
  - Child 2 – O
  - Child 3 – G
- When you get to the end of the word the next child (Child 4) says
  'Buzz off!' to the child sitting next to them (Child 5). This child (Child
  5) is then out and sits down.
- You then read aloud a new word and show a visual card and carry on
  with the next child (Child 6).

- If any of the children get part of the spelling incorrect, they have to sit out and the opportunity to guess the letter goes to the next child.
- Carry on like this until two children are standing and they spell a word between them. The one who says 'Buzz off!' wins.

Suitable for

Any Key Stage

Variations

- You could do this activity in pairs to start with, so that the EAL pupil(s) have a support system to help them.
- You could show the word on the interactive white board then hide it so that the children saw the word before they needed to spell it. The child who is buzzed off and didn't spell the word can reveal it at the end so they don't feel as if they didn't have a chance to take part.

English - Word wheel

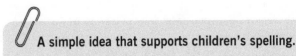

A simple idea that supports children's spelling.

Aims

- To recognise spelling patterns
- To increase vocabulary lists
- BIC

Vocabulary

Any words that have letter blend

Resources

- Scissors
- Card
- Compass or something to draw around for a circle
- Pencils/pens
- Butterfly fasteners for the centre of the circles
- Dictionary

What to do

- Ask each child to draw and cut out two different-sized circles. The smaller circle will fit into the larger one.
- Provide the children with a letter blend that they are going to look at, for example flor, st. They then write this on the smaller wheel.
- On the larger circle they write a selection of blends or endings that would go with that blend, for example ick, ock, eak.

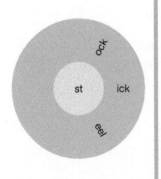

- They then fix the two circles together and rotate the larger circle so that they create various words.
- The children then create a story, poem or list of the various words they can make with.

Suitable for

Any Key Stage

Variations

- Create a rhyming wheel using the same strategy then make a rhyming story, or poem with words that have the same sound or spelling.

English - Discuss and decide!

A group activity that encourages reasoning and discussion about particular issues.

Aims

- To read, discuss and decide upon answers to a particular question
- To justify opinion
- CALP

Vocabulary

Language related to reasoning, justification, evaluation

Resources

- A pack for each group that contains:
  A set of 16 cards with responses to a question
  A question card

What to do

- Organise the class into mixed-ability threes and place the EAL pupil in the middle of the group.
- Provide them with a set of cards that contain statements that could potentially answer a question or resolve an issue, such as 'Why did the fire of London get out of control?'
- The pupils have to read the cards and discuss which they think are relevant and which are not. They put the ones that are irrelevant to one side.
- Next they put the other cards in rank order so that the statement they think is most relevant to the question will be at the top of the list. They MUST discuss why they have this order and which statement is most likely to be the answer to the question.
- Finally bring the class back together and discuss what they have as their reasons and why.

Example

Many people had the plague and were not well enough to help with the fire	The houses were too tall	The fire equipment was not advanced enough to cope with such a large fire	There were too many stray dogs
It started in Pudding Lane	The houses were too close together	It hadn't rained for a while	London was a long way from the sea
Many people didn't believe the fire had started	There was a north-westerly wind	It was difficult to find the Mayor	It started in a bakery
The people were frightened	The buildings were made of wood	It was night time	People were asleep

Suitable for

KS2, KS3

Variations

- This activity idea can be used with any issue, such as:
    Is it right that fox hunting was banned?
    Why did the earthquake in Haiti happen?
    Should children start school at age 4?
    Why do people follow a religion?

Mathematics - Buzz Fizz! Fizz Buzz!

A fun class multiplication game that is good for filling in time! It should be conducted at quite a fast pace.

Aims

- To reinforce knowledge of multiplication patterns
- CALP

Vocabulary

Mathematical vocabulary
Multiplication
Multiplied
Times

Resources

- Possibly a number square on an interactive white board as a visual aid

What to do

- Explain that they are going to count in ones but recognise certain multiples
- The children take it in turns to count one by one but when they reach a certain multiple they have to say BUZZ instead of the number.
  For example – we are to recognise multiples of 5:

      Child A – 1
      Child B – 2
      Child C – 3
      Child D – 4
      Child E – BUZZ!
- To make it more complicated add Fizz into the situation and say we are now also going to recognise multiples of 3 and we will say FIZZ instead of that number:

      Child A – 1
      Child B – 2

> Child C – FIZZ!
> Child D – 4
> Child E – BUZZ!
> Child F – FIZZ!
> Child G – 7
> Child H – 8
> - When they get to multiples of both, such as 15, they say BUZZ FIZZ!

Suitable for

Mainly KS2, KS3 yet can be simplified for KS1

Variations

- This can become even more complicated by adding more conditions, e.g. whenever the number includes a digit that has 5 or 3 then the children have to recognise it alongside its multiple. For example:

  15 would be 1 and BUZZ,

  25 would be 2 and BUZZ,

  13 would be 1 and FIZZ etc.

  When you get to 30, which is a multiple of both and contains a 3, you would say FIZZY BUZZ FIZZ! or something similar to recognise its complexity.

Mathematics - XOXO

A fun game for pairs that involves problem solving and strategic thinking.

Aims

- To think logically
- BIC/CALP

Vocabulary

Your turn
Oh no!
You got me!
I win!
Rules

Resources

- XOXO grid and pencils

What to do

- Provide a XOXO grid like the one overleaf and place the pupils in mixed-ability pairs. One child is X and the other is O.
- The aim of the game is to get from one side of the board to the other without being stopped by your opponent: X moves from bottom to top and O from left to right. You cannot cross your opponent's path.
- The pupils take it in turns to move one move at a time: O goes first.

- The winner is the person who reaches the other side first.

```
X         X         X         X         X

     O         O         O         O         O

X         X         X         X         X

     O         O         O         O         O

X         X         X         X         X

     O         O         O         O         O

X         X         X         X         X

     O         O         O         O         O
```

Suitable for

KS1, KS2

Variations

None

Mathematics – Guess my hand!

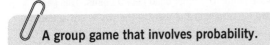

A group game that involves probability.

Aims

- To develop understanding of probability
- To develop social skills and play in a group
- To practise speaking in a group situation
- BIC

Vocabulary

Numbers
Sentence: 'I think there are X counters in total'

Resources

- About four counters for each pupil that can be held neatly in the hand.

What to do

- Place your pupils in mixed-ability groups of four and give them a set of counters (about four each).
- Each player chooses a number of counters to hold in their right hand and a number in their left hand. They do not tell anyone the number they are holding in either hand.
- When ready, they each put their closed right hand on the table, and one by one in a clockwise direction, decide how many counters are likely to be in total in the hands on the table (they are not allowed to guess the same number). They say the sentence 'I think there are X counters in total.'
- Once everyone has guessed the total number of counters, they all open their hands and count. Whoever is closest to the real total wins that round and sits out. They gain 3 points. They then watch whilst the other three play again.

- This happens until the last two children are playing and the final child wins and gets 1 point. The other child gets 0 points. This game continues with three more rounds and then all the scores are added up for an overall winner.
- It is useful to reinforce the learning about probability in a structured plenary or group discussion at the end of the four rounds.

Suitable for

Any Key Stage

Variations

None

Science - Classification

In science we like to use tree diagrams to classify plants, animals etc. This is a simple activity that requires the children to classify minibeasts.

Aims

- To classify minibeasts
- To be able to discuss the characteristics of certain minibeasts
- To use descriptive language
- BIC/CALP

Vocabulary

Names of minibeasts: worm, grasshopper, dragonfly, ladybird, ant, butterfly, honeybee, millipede, stag beetle, slug, ground beetle, wasp, centipede, woodlouse, spider, snail

Resources

- Laminated images or drawings of the minibeasts
- Laminated classification key sheets
- Examples of these can be found in Appendix 2

What to do

- Place the pupils in mixed-ability twos or threes and give each group a laminated classification key sheet and a set of cards. The EAL pupil(s) holds the cards.
- Model what to do and then ask them to have a go with their classification game.
- As a team the children look at the drawing/image of a minibeast and, using the classification key sheet, work out what it is, some of its characteristics and what it does.

Suitable for

KS1

Variations

- This can be adapted to classify a set of mathematical objects, geographical features etc. and is a good EAL activity because of the language that it stimulates.

Science - Language lab coat

A simple idea that embeds and extends scientific vocabulary and can be used as an assessment tool.

Aims

- To develop and extend scientific vocabulary
- BIC/CALP

Vocabulary

Scientific terms related to the attainment targets in the National Curriculum

Resources

- A white shirt
- Fabric pens
- Felt tips
- Permanent markers

What to do

- Ask each child to bring in from home an old white adult-sized men's shirt that will be his/her lab coat for Science lessons.
- Direct all the children to draw their name with an image on the breast pocket and hang it up in class for future use.
- Whenever they have used and learnt new vocabulary for a topic, such as the parts of a flower, they prove they know it by relaying it to you and then writing the words with a corresponding image on their lab coat. They can draw and write anywhere they wish. Encourage them to use brightly coloured felt tips, permanent markers or fabric paint.
- Keep adding new vocabulary and drawings to the coat throughout the year so that it ends up with drawings, words and brightly coloured scientific diagrams all over it. It will become a visual document that shows what they know, understand and can do in Science. It will also become a record of what they have learnt over the year.

Suitable for

Any Key Stage

Variations

None

Science - Make a floating compass

The pupils work together to make a floating compass.

Aims

- To make a simple compass
- To learn the concept of direction
- CALP

Vocabulary

Magnetise
Magnetism
Magnetic north
Instructions

Resources

(Per group)
- Magnet
- Needle
- Cork
- Water
- Bowl
- Visual and written instructions
- Paper clip
- Globe

What to do

- Place the pupils in mixed-ability twos or threes and model what they will do.
- Give them all the materials they need and ask them to make a compass, using the visual instructions to support the written instructions.
  - Rub the needle (many times) lengthwise along the magnet to magnetise it.
  - Test to see if the needle is magnetised by trying to use it to pick up a paper clip. If it doesn't pick it up you need to rub for a little longer.
  - Push the needle lengthwise through the cork (USE AN ADULT TO HELP FOR SAFETY REASONS).
  - Place it in a bowl of water and slightly spin the cork. Watch it to see when it stops turning. Turn it again and see if it stops in the same place.
  - If it stops in the same place then it is pointing to magnetic north. Use a compass to see if this is true!

Suitable for

KS2, KS3 and can be used for KS1 with support for safety and related questioning

Variations

- This can be extended for Geography, and to stimulate discussion of why knowing about magnetic north is important for navigation.

ICT - Crazy Talk!

A hilarious downloadable program that allows children to manipulate a picture or photograph so that the character speaks!

Aims

- To use technology to create a speaking character
- To create a voiceover for a character
- To write, speak and record the voice for a character
- BIC/CALP

Vocabulary

General conversational language

Resources

- *CrazyTalk* software http://www.reallusion.com/crazytalk/
- Digital camera or a photograph/picture that has been scanned

What to do

- Place your pupils in mixed-ability groups of three and provide them with a computer that has the *CrazyTalk* software (there is a free download to 'play' with but for the finished file to be saved you would need to purchase the program).
- The pupils choose a character from the list provided on the program.
- Together they write a short script for the character. It can be based on the class topic or a general conversation about themselves. For example, if the character is a dog then a script about what the dog likes to do.
- Using the *CrazyTalk* software the children provide the character with a mouth and facial expressions etc.

- They then perform the script and record their voice using the *CrazyTalk* software so that the character's lips move to the same speed and rhythm as the recorded voice.
- Finally they watch the clip and then show their character to the rest of the class. It is useful to use this part of the project/session to evaluate how to improve the end product.

Suitable for

Any Key Stage but will need adult support for KS1

Variations

- *CrazyTalk* can be used to manipulate a picture or photograph. The children could provide an image of Henry VIII, for example, and create a monologue, or they could take a photograph of themselves and manipulate it so that they speak in each other's voices.

ICT - Interactive Teaching Programs

A bank of resources that can support a variety of lessons but in particular the Core subjects.

Aims

- To use technology to support learning
- For EAL pupils to learn through multimedia
- BIC/CALP

Vocabulary

Language related to the subject

Resources

- Broadband
- PC
- ITPs downloaded and saved in the shared areas on desktops

What to do

- Interactive Teaching Programs (ITPs) are fantastic resources for supporting learning because they translate abstract concepts into concrete terms through a visual medium. They are mainly used for interactive white boards but can also be used on PCs at home and in a classroom. They are good for EAL pupils as they require some form of interaction and, if used effectively, can enhance learning and teaching.
  - A guide to ITPs http://nationalstrategies.standards.dcsf.gov.uk/node/64592
  - BBC Schools link to many ITPs and educational material http://www.bbc.co.uk/schools
  - A list of ITPs mainly for Mathematics but including ITPs for English http://nationalstrategies.standards.dcsf.gov.uk/search/primary/results/nav:49909

- English http://www.bbc.co.uk/schools/magickey
- History http://www.ancientegypt.co.uk/menu.html
- Science http://www.nhm.ac.uk/kids-only
- Geography at KS1 http://www.bbc.co.uk/schools/barnabybear/
- RE for Early Years http://www.dottieandbuzz.co.uk/
- RE, Art, History, Culture http://www.bl.uk/learning/cult/sacredbooks/sacredintro.html
- There are many more ITPs available to support learning. They can be used creatively to help EAL learners access the curriculum and many are free!

Suitable for

Any Key Stage

Variations

None

History - Let's pretend!

A fun activity that can be recreated for any historical situation and requires imagination and confidence to act in role.

Aims

- To empathise with people who experienced a historical event
- To develop confidence and language capabilities to act in role
- CALP

Vocabulary

Vocabulary related to the topic, such as gas mask, air raid, shelter, evacuation, role play, ration book etc.

Resources

- Dressing-up clothes
- Items that are related to the period of study, e.g. gas masks etc.
- Large hall
- Blacked-out windows in classroom

What to do

- The children recreate a time and event in history using role play, then discuss the emotions of the character they were playing. For example:

  SCENARIO – They are at home and the air-raid siren goes off. They have to find shelter. Do they rush to the air-raid shelter or stay at home? What makes them decide?

  The children are given different roles and are placed in family groups, e.g.:
  - Air raid officials
  - Home Guards

- Evacuated children
- Parents
- Shopkeepers
- A spy or two etc.

They then put on costumes or some item of clothing that is appropriate to their character and re-enact what it would have been like during this time. They start the role play in the school hall.

When the children begin their role play they are in a normal family situation but then the alarm goes off (it's a good idea to have an example to play) and they have to remain in character and decide whether to stay in the hall or go to the classroom. The classroom is the air-raid shelter and is blacked out.

After they have conducted the role play place the children in groups equivalent to their roles and ask them to discuss how they felt as that character and what they did. Then discuss as a class.

- After the role play it is always useful to consolidate the learning with videos, trips to museums and English tasks such as writing diaries, letters etc. as if they are in role.

Suitable for

KS2, KS3. Historical role play is also suitable for KS1, if the scenario is adapted.

Variations

- The role play can either take place with each family group acting at the same time (which is a little chaotic) or one at a time with the rest of the class watching. I prefer the chaotic approach to start with, as this creates more of an atmosphere.

History - Archaeological artefacts

The children become archaeologists for a day and hypothesise about the significance of what they find.

Aims

- To create questions
- To work as a team to hypothesise about an artefact
- To develop language related to historical inquiry
- CALP

Vocabulary

Object
Archaeologist
Artefact
Old
Purpose

Resources

- A selection of props such as magnifying glasses, hats, scarves, brushes etc.
- A clipboard with paper and pencil to record what they find
- Artefacts (that can be broken completely or partially) that will be buried and investigated, e.g.

an old toy	a plate	a coin	jewellery
a comb	a shoe	an ornament	an old fork
a belt	a buckle	a key	a glass bottle

What to do

- In a large sand pit or ideally in a soil bed outside, bury a selection of artefacts (they can be broken) for the children to dig up. It may be better to leave them over the weekend in the soil bed so that they are not too easily found. Make a map of where each artefact is so that you don't forget!
- Group the children in mixed-ability threes or fours and explain that they are archaeologists and they are to discover some possible hidden gems.
- A teaching assistant or other adult takes the groups one by one to the soil pit and asks them to become archaeologists and find their artefact. They have to use the brushes and trowels carefully to find it.
- Once they have found an artefact, they return to the class and consider what they know about the artefact and hypothesise about its significance. It may be useful to provide a worksheet such as the one below.
- They then list questions that they want to ask about it.

Draw the artefact you have found:	Describe exactly where you found it and what it looks like:	
	Who do you think it belonged to and how did they use it?	
	How was it made?	
	Is it valuable?	
	How old do you think it is?	
	What is it made from?	
	Where might you find others like it?	
	What do you want to know about your object?	1. 2. 3. 4. 5.

Suitable for

Any Key Stage

Variations

- If you have a big enough area in school take the whole class out at the same time and set them to find their artefact.
- Invite an archaeologist into school to talk about their finds.
- Visit a museum or have a museum visit you to look at artefacts that have been discovered.
- Turn this into a history mystery where they have to sort the objects and discuss which objects were dropped, left or thrown away.

Geography - Gardening glory

This idea can become a huge project, but its essence is to design and create a class indoor or outdoor edible garden. It's a good idea to start this in late winter or early spring ready for crops in the summer.

Aims

- To understand that plants can be grown to eat
- To grow edible plants
- BIC/CALP

Vocabulary

Eco-friendly
Edible
Names of plants
Food
Soil, pots
Food miles

Resources

- Bags of compost
- Seeds for edible plants, including potatoes
- Large containers
- Gardening spades
- Herb plants

What to do

- As a class contact a garden centre and ask if they would donate some gardening produce for your class of children as part of their community links policy. If they do not donate anything, then you may have to raise some money for this project.

- Decide as a class what they would like to grow and why (depending on your space) and then divide the class into mixed-ability groups of threes. Give each group two types of plants that they will plant and become responsible for.
- The children care for their crops and whilst waiting for them to grow take part in a selection of group literacy activities such as those listed in the table below.
- Once ready, harvest the crop and have a class meal and end of term party.

Create a report card of when the crop is watered and how much is given.	Look into how to keep pests away and test out various methods.
Write a list with images of what sort of meals you could make with your crop.	Look at food miles and research why it is better to shop local.
Write a set of instructions on how to care for the crop.	Design a seed packet for your crop.

Suitable for

Any Key Stage

Variations

- It would be lovely to take the children to a local garden centre or allotment and have a talk with the gardeners there to get some tips on how to grow food.
- You could visit a local supermarket to find out where the food they sell comes from – local versus global – and discuss food miles etc.
- You could visit a local allotment and ask gardeners about their crop rotations etc.
- Compare the food that can be grown in the UK with the t food that is and can be grown in the home countries/continents of the EAL pupil(s) in your class.
- Get parents involved as part of the 'Big Society' and create a community allotment on your school grounds. See **http://www.landshare.net** for more information about creating community projects.

Geography - Where is it from?

A fun activity that inspires discussion about localities and social geography.

Aims

- To begin to consider how people live in different parts of the world, and their culture
- To be aware of stereotyping
- To use an artefact to inspire research into localities
- CALP

Vocabulary

Hats
Country, continent, custom
Stereotype
Place, locality
Names of places around the world
Special, occasion, everyday

Resources

- A selection of hats that are worn in particular places and are used both for special occasions and for everyday wear
- A selection of hat boxes
- Sealed envelopes that contain information about the hats and localities

What to do

- Give each small mixed-ability group a hat box. Inside they find a hat and a sealed envelope. The hats are from around the world, e.g. a sombrero, a turban, a deerstalker, a beret, a kippa etc., and the sealed envelope contains information about the country/ continent the hat comes from.

- The pupils are not permitted to open the envelope yet but are encouraged to discuss in their groups where they think the hat is from, who would wear it, when they would wear it and why they would wear it.
- They then have to think of three questions they would like to ask about the country/continent that the hat is likely to come from.
- They are then allowed to open their envelope and read what it says about their hat.
- They finally share their ideas and questions as a class and you discuss the danger of stereotyping people and places, e.g. not everyone in France wears a beret.

Suitable for

Any Key Stage

Variations

- The hats could belong to actual people from the suggested localities and the children could write to them/email them and find out more about their home.
- The children could research and answer their three questions by using texts, encyclopaedias and suggested websites to create a poster about their locality and its customs.

PE - Be a bean!

A fun and popular warm-up game that uses language to create movement.

Aims

- To extend basic vocabulary
- To raise the heart rate
- BIC

Vocabulary

Broad bean
Beanstalk
Jelly bean
Runner bean
Jumping bean
Baked bean
Frozen bean
Run
Stop

Resources

- A loud voice – and/or a tambourine or whistle to gain attention
- A set of cards that show the image of a bean and the action that goes with it

What to do

- The children run around in a safe manner, dodging in and out of each other.
- When you gain their attention (with a whistle or tambourine) you shout the name of a bean and hold up the corresponding visual card.
- The children then have to do that action until you say 'BEANS GO!' and they continue to run around the room/playground again.

- Eventually you will not need the visual aids, but they are useful to start with.

Broad bean	Stretch arms and legs as wide as possible
Beanstalk	Stretch arms up and point fingers. Stand on tiptoe
Jelly bean	Wobble arms, legs and body
Runner bean	Run on the spot
Jumping bean	Do star jumps on the spot
Frozen bean	Freeze in the last position and stand as still as possible
Baked bean	Lie flat on the floor

Suitable for

KS1, KS2

Variations

- The children create their own list with actions and cards for warm-up. This can be in the home languages of the children in your class.
- You could eventually shout out a different bean to the card you hold up but the children have to do the shouted action not the visual one.
- Instead of actions with beans you could warm up with the popular pirates activity where the children have to do actions related to pirates such as walk the plank, fire the cannons etc.

PE - Peer perfect

A simple idea that helps pupils refine gymnastic balances and learn with and from each other.

Aims

- To get children to work together and in different groups
- To refine balances and create a sequence
- BIC

Vocabulary

Balance
Points (small areas of the body such as fingers, toes, knees)
Patches (large areas of the body such as back, bottom)
Toes
Group
Numbers
Sequence

Resources

- A whistle or tambourine to gain attention
- Mats for safety
- Safe clothing and no shoes or socks

What to do

- The children run around to warm up (and possibly play a warm-up game such as 'Be a bean'.)
- When you shout a number and hold up the corresponding visual aid the children have to form a group that has the same number of children as is on the card. They then have to create a balance as a group using patches and points.

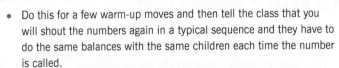

- Do this for a few warm-up moves and then tell the class that you will shout the numbers again in a typical sequence and they have to do the same balances with the same children each time the number is called.
- Ensure that every time they are doing the balance they refine it so that they point toes, hold still etc.

Suitable for

KS1, KS2

Variations

- You could call out the numbers in one of the home languages in the class.
- You could extend the activity so that they balance on two patches and one point within the group etc.

Art and DT - Making clothes

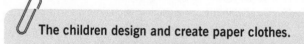

The children design and create paper clothes.

Aims

- To work collaboratively to create a design and finished product
- To develop language related to evaluation, reasoning, justification
- CALP

Vocabulary

Language related to materials (soft, hard, rough, patterned, manipulate, pliable)
Language related to evaluation, justification and reasoning

Resources

- Different sizes and colours of paper including newspaper and card
- Glue, staple clips and staplers, fasteners, Sellotape
- Pens, pencils
- Paint

What to do

- Place the children in mixed-ability groups of four and give them a design brief such as:

  You have to create an outfit for a pop star. It MUST be made out of paper and card. You can use other items to decorate it such as glitter, paint, sequins etc.

- The children have to design the item and consider how to make it out of newspaper or scrap paper such as the old advertising paper that used to be on billboards (you can get materials from the scrap and recycle banks that some local authorities have set up for schools).

- The children use the card to create a structure for the clothing and then rub the paper so that it becomes soft and more pliable and use this for the cloth. They can fasten with Sellotape, staples or glue, but the child who models the clothes must be able to step out of them without ripping them.
- At the end of the project, ask the children to write up their brief and design, and then present their outfit and designs to a special assembly.

Suitable for

KS2, KS3

Variations

- This can be adapted so that the brief is related to their topic, such as a coat for a Tudor king or a dress for a child in the 1930s etc.

Art and DT - Drawing blindfolded

A simple idea that requires listening to another's instructions and trying to draw what they say.

Aims

- To be able to describe an object/subject
- To listen and respond in a visual way
- BIC/CALP

Vocabulary

Describing words

Resources

- A set of cards with subjects to draw
- Pens
- Pencils
- Paper

What to do

- Divide the pupils up in friendship and/or mixed-ability pairs and give them a set of cards that have things to draw on them such as dog, house, horse, car, etc and pencils and paper. They are named A or B.
- A goes first and B is blindfolded. A takes the card from the top of the pile and describes it to B, who has to draw it. They tell them exactly what to draw and how, e.g. long line, circle above the line etc, but they are not permitted to use the name of the thing they are drawing. They have one minute to draw the subject.
- Once the minute is up they take off the blindfold and show the drawing. It is then B's turn to have a go.

Suitable for

Any Key Stage

Variations

- Place the pupils in mixed-ability table groups and play as a competition against the other tables.
- Both children are blindfolded and a third child describes what to draw.
- Play the game *Pictionary!*

Art and DT - Squiggle stories

One child draws a squiggle on a piece of paper and the other creates a masterpiece.

Aims

- To think creatively
- To be able to describe what they have drawn
- To be able to recount a tale/story based on their squiggle
- CALP

Vocabulary

Descriptive language

Resources

- Paper
- Pens
- Pencils

What to do

- Divide the pupils into mixed-ability friendship pairs and provide each pupil with a large piece of paper and pens.
- Child A draws a squiggle for Child B on a piece of paper and Child B creates one for Child A on another piece.
- Each child has to create something from that squiggle. They have five minutes to draw.
- Once the five minutes are up they have to think up a story/tale related to the squiggle and relay it to their partner.
- The retelling could be part of a plenary to the rest of the class.

Suitable for

Any Key Stage

Variations

- Do this as a class lesson, where you draw a squiggle, another child makes it into something and then the whole class create a story related to it.
- You draw a squiggle for each child and tell them what you want them to create, e.g. a monster, building, object for sitting on, holiday scene etc.

Music - Walking with sound

A wonderful idea that brings the sound of the outside into the music classroom.

Aims

- To create a piece of music related to sounds from their locality
- To use describing words and develop a vocabulary list
- CALP

Vocabulary

A set of describing words
Unison
Collective nouns and names of instruments
Onomatopoeic words
Orchestra
Perform

Resources

- Paper, clipboard and pencils for walk
- A digital recorder (optional)
- A large selection of percussion instruments
- Pictures of the things that made the sounds, e.g. a bird, bus, car etc.

What to do

- Take the children on a short walk around their locality. At certain points in the walk, stop and ask the children to listen to the sounds that they can hear.
- In mixed-ability threes they jot down on their sheet (visually or in words) what they hear, e.g. a bus, a bird, swishing of the wind in the trees. They try to describe what it sounds like. Encourage the use of onomatopoeia.

- Back in class the children have an opportunity to look at a variety of instruments and decide which percussion instruments suit certain sounds.
- Divide the walk up between the groups (it might be useful to join the groups into groups of six) and ask each group to create the sounds that they heard for that section. Encourage them to use the instruments in unison and individually.
- They perform the sections in order to each other and then discuss how to refine and record each section so that they become an orchestra and perform as a class.

Suitable for

KS1, KS2

Music - Sing out like a bell!

A fun activity that requires team work to create a bell-ringing composition although no bell is used!

Aims

- To work as a team
- To develop musical vocabulary
- BIC

Vocabulary

Bell
Peal
Pitch
Bell sounds – onomatopoeia – dang, dong, ping, ding, dring, bong etc.

Resources

- A bank of words for the bell sounds (optional)
- A recording of a peal of bells, or visit a church and listen

What to do

- As a warm-up go around the class and ask each child to make a sound like a bell. List the various words that can make a bell sound such as BING, BONG, DONG, DING, PING. Discuss how bell sounds can have various pitches and levels of loudness.
- Listen to a peal of bells and note how they have a certain rhythm and sequence.
- Divide the class into mixed-ability groups of four and set them the task of creating a peal of bells using only their voice. They have to work as a team and agree on sound, pitch, loudness and order.
- Finally each group performs their peal.

Suitable for

KS1, KS2

Variations

- Include body movements with the bell sounds, e.g. a large deep sound may have a body shape that is large and a high-pitched sound may be tall and thin.
- Practise putting their bell sounds into order or pitch, e.g. high to low.
- Link the peal to a Religious Education topic about celebrations.

Religious Education - Filmed footage

A selection of filmed resources that can make RE more inspiring.

Aims

- To use a selection of the clips at the start or in the middle of a lesson to promote discussion
- To create questions that they wish to find the answers to
- To develop confidence to speak in a pair and then as a member of a larger group
- CALP

Vocabulary

Question, answer
Talk partners
What, why, where, who, when, how

Resources

- Filmed footage using the search engine within the websites
  Class Clips – http://www.bbc.co.uk/learningzone/clips
  YouTube – http://www.youtube.com (be careful as some of the clips are for an adult audience or are biased; however, you can get some good clips of religious practice)

What to do

- Divide up your pupils into mixed-ability talk partners.
- Explain what the clip is about and ask the pairs to come up with a question they would like answered, based on the theme. For example, if you are going to show a clip of a baptism, what question do they want to find the answer to? Ask them to write it on a white board.

- Show the clip and then ask the pupils to pair up with another pair (so that now they are a group of four) and discuss whether their question was answered. If it wasn't answered, is the other pair able to answer it?
- The four now join another four to make a group of eight and share their questions and answers. Again, if they still do not have an answer to their question can anyone else in the group answer it?
- As a class, discuss what they asked and the answers they got. List the answers by either sticking their white boards onto the wall with Blu-Tack or writing the questions on a board. Any unanswered questions become a focus for the next set of learning about the topic.

Suitable for

Any Key Stage

Variations

None

Religious Education – Question Time

Children interview a selection of visitors using the style of the BBC TV discussion show *Question Time*.

Aims

- To work as a team to research and compose a question to ask a panel of experts
- To gain confidence to direct a question to a panel of experts
- CALP

Vocabulary

Religious and topic language associated with the area being discussed

Resources

- Broadband and textbooks for research
- Table and chairs
- Water for panel

What to do

- Invite three or four people to become an expert panel similar to *Question Time*.
- Before the speakers visit the school, prepare the pupils so that they understand who the visitors are and the purpose of their visit.
- BEFORE the visit, divide the pupils into groups and ask them to research specific areas that will be useful when interviewing the visitors, e.g. if one is a person from the Islamic community a group could research and compose three questions and information material about
  - practice
  - clothing
  - pilgrimage
  - sacred space.

- Look through the questions and as a class decide (using 'Corner running' if you wish: see Chapter 4) which questions they will definitely ask and then allocate the questions to volunteers.
- ON THE DAY OF THE VISIT organise the classroom so that there is a table at the front of the class for the panel (it is always nice to do this in the hall) and the chairs are arranged so that there is an audience.
- Choose one or two confident pupils to be the equivalent to Jonathan Dimbleby, who will field the questions and direct the discussion (with your support).
- The children take turns to ask questions and the panel to answer from their perspective. Allow a lot of time for discussion and encourage personal opinion.

Suitable for

KS2, KS3

Variations

- Rather than a panel of people you could invite one person and conduct the visit in a similar way to journalistic interviews on programmes such as *Newsround* or the *BBC News*. The questions will have been created by the class in advance of the interview but one or two children would ask them. This could be filmed or recorded and placed on the school website.
- The visitor could be in a 'hot seat' and the children take it in turns to ask questions.

Religious Education - Loop game!

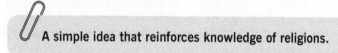

A simple idea that reinforces knowledge of religions.

Aims

- To develop confidence to read English aloud
- To improve their basic knowledge about facts in RE (AT1)
- To develop religious vocabulary
- BIC/CALP

Vocabulary

Technical vocabulary related to RE

Resources:

- Loop game cards laminated and cut up
- A master sheet for you to refer to

What to do

- Group the pupils in mixed-ability pairs and give them one or two cards from the loop game sheet (see below).
- Go over what the cards say with each pair, then start the loop.
- The pair that hold the START card read their card aloud: *Who wears a kippa on their head?*
- The children check their cards and if they have the answer, they read it aloud and then ask the question which is on their card.
- They continue like this until they get to the END card (see the loop game below).

Suitable for

KS2, KS3

- If the children are unsure whether they have the correct answer ask them to have a guess then help with the answer. It is a good idea, however, to practise this game a few times to see if they get quicker each time. This way they will eventually remember the facts.

START Who wears a kippa on their head? END I am Christianity	I am a Jew Who is the head of the Roman Catholic Church?	I am the Pope Who believes that wine in the communion is the **actual blood** of Christ when it has been blessed?	I am a Roman Catholic Who wears five items on their body, which are called the 5Ks, to show they belong to their faith?
I am a Sikh Who uses Mala beads to meditate?	I am a Buddhist Who worships a god called Ganesh?	I am a Hindu What is the name of the Hindu festival of lights?	I am Diwali Who is believed to be married to the Hindu god Sita?
I am the god Rama Who was betrothed to Joseph?	I am Mary What is the Jewish sacred text called?	I am The Torah Who prays five times a day?	I am a Muslim Which sacred text is recognised and read by Judaism and Christianity?
I am the Old Testament What is the name of the Buddhist sacred space?	I am a temple What is the name of the Jewish sacred space?	I am a synagogue What is the name of the Islamic sacred space?	I am a mosque What is the name of the Islamic festival of fasting for 30 days?
I am Ramadan What is the name of the Christian spring festival that remembers Jesus' death?	I am Easter What is the name of the Christian sacred space?	I am a church What is the Jewish festival that happens on a Friday evening and ends on a Saturday evening called?	I am the Sabbath What is a mezuzah?

I am a box on a Jewish doorpost and contain the Shema What is the Shema?	I am the Jewish holy rule What is the Christian Great Commandment?	I am Love your neighbour as you love yourself Who gave Jesus a gift of gold?	I am a wise man Who told Mary in the Christian story that she was pregnant with Jesus Christ?
I am the angel Gabriel Who carried Mary to Bethlehem?	I am the donkey What is the name of the artefact used to hold the wine in Christian ceremonies?	I am a chalice What is the name of the Indian festival were people throw powder paint at each other?	I am Holi What is the name of the ceremony for a boy's initiation into the Jewish faith?
I am Bar Mitzvah Which religion has a sacred thread ceremony?	I am Hinduism Which religion follows the Eightfold Path?	I am Buddhism Which religion has five rules which are called pillars?	I am Islam Which religion has ten commandments?

Variations

- The game can be used for one religion rather than for many as in the example. It can also be an assessment tool or used as a plenary where you want to reinforce AT1 and the specific facts they have looked at in the lesson.
- Consider using loop games in other areas. They are good for many subjects, not just RE and Maths.

Further reading

August, D., Shanahan, T. (eds) (2008) 'Developing literacy in second language learners: report of the National Literacy Panel on language-minority children and youth', in 'Book reviews', *International Journal of Bilingual Education and Bilingualism*, 11: 1, 107–113.

Baker, C. (2001) *Foundations of Bilingual Education and Bilingualism*, 3rd edn., Clevedon: Multilingual Matters Ltd.

Baker, C. (2007) *A Parents' and Teachers' Guide to Bilingualism*, 3rd edn., Clevedon: Multilingual Matters Ltd.

Baker, C. and Hornberger, N.H. (2001) *An Introductory Reader to the Writings of Jim Cummins*, Clevedon: Multilingual Matters Ltd.

Bakhsh, Q., Harding, E. and Vaughan, C. (1985) *Teaching the Bilingual Child. The Gravesend Study of a Bilingual Approach to Teaching the English Language to Infants*, Commission of Racial Equality.

Claire, E. (2004) *ESL Teacher's Activities Kit*, Harlow: Prentice Hall Publishers.

Collins, Lucy (1999) *Maisy's Mix and Match Mousewear. 216 different outfits*, London: Walker Books.

Crosse, K. (2007) *Introducing English as an Additional Language to Young Children: A Practical Handbook*, London: Paul Chapman Publishing.

Cummins, James (1979) 'Linguistic Interdependence and the Educational Development of Bilingual Children', *Review of Educational Research* 49:3, pp. 222–51.

Cummins, J. (2000) *Language, Power and Pedagogy*, Clevedon: Multilingual Matters Ltd.

Cummins, J. and Gibbons, P. (2002) *Scaffolding Language, Scaffolding Learning: Teaching Second Language Learners in the Mainstream Classroom*, Portsmouth: Heinemann.

Dash, N. (2007) *Teaching English as an Additional Language*, New Delhi: Atlantic Publishers and Distributors.

Einhorn, K. (2001) *Easy and Engaging ESL Activities and Mini-Books for Every Classroom*, Teaching Resources.

Frassler, R. (2003) *Room for Talk: Teaching and Learning in a Multilingual Kindergarten*, London: Teachers College Press.

Garcia, O. (2009) *Bilingual Education in the 21st Century: A Global Perspective*, Chichester: Wiley-Blackwell Publishing.

Garcia, O. and Baker, C. (2007) *Bilingual Education: An Introductory Reader*, Clevedon: Multilingual Matters Ltd.

Gardner, H. (1999) *Intelligence Reframed: Multiple Intelligences for the 21st Century*, New York: Basic Books.

Gutteridge, Daphne and Smith, Viv (2008) *Using Circle Time for PSHE and Citizenship: A Year's Plan for KS2 Teachers*, London: David Foulton Publishers.

Gutteridge, Daphne and Smith, Viv (2009) *Creating an Emotionally Healthy Classroom*, London: David Foulton Publishers.

Haslam, L., Wilkin, Y. and Kellet, E. (2004) *English as an Additional Language: Meeting the Challenge in the Classroom*, London: David Foulton Publishers.

Institute of Education (2009) *Teaching EAL: Four Priorities of the Development of English as Additional Language (EAL) Workforce in Schools (Supporting Evidence)*, TDA.

Leat, David and Nichols, Adam (1999) *Theory into Practice: Mysteries Make You Think*, Sheffield: Geographical Association.

Leung, C. and Creese, A., NALDIC (2010) *English as an Additional Language: A Guide for Teachers Working with Linguistic Minority Pupils*, London: Sage Publications.

QCA (1999) *The National Curriculum Handbook for Primary Teachers in England*, London: DfEE.

Rule, F. (2008) *The Worst Street in London*, Hersham, Surrey: Ian Allan Publishing.

Scott, C. (2008) *Teaching Children English as an Additional Language: A Programme for 7–12 Year Olds*, Abingdon: Routledge.

Sharratt, Nick (1994) *Ketchup On Your Cornflakes?* London: Scholastic Children's Books.

Smyth, G. (2003) *Helping Bilingual Pupils to Access the Curriculum*, London: David Foulton Publishers.

Vygotsky, L. (1978), *Mind in Society*, Cambridge, Mass: Harvard University Press.

Webster, M. (2010) *Creative Approaches to Teaching Primary RE*, Harlow: Pearson Education Ltd.

Websites

EAL pupils and literacy hour
http://nationalstrategies.standards.dcsf.gov.uk/node/85095

Ethnic Minority Achievement Grant http://www.qcda.gov.uk/7278.aspx
(accessed 22.09.09)

Ethnic Minority Achievement Support Services – do a web search for
EMASS (such as with Google or Bing) and you will find many local
authority websites that have resources and information, for example
http://www.milton-keynes.gov.uk/emass

Interactive Teaching Programmes

A guide to ITPs
http://nationalstrategies.standards.dcsf.gov.uk/node/64592
BBC Schools link to many ITPs and educational material http://www.bbc.co.uk/
schools

A list of ITPs mainly for Mathematics, but including ITPs for English
http://nationalstrategies.standards.dcsf.gov.uk/search/primary/results/nav:49909

English
http://www.bbc.co.uk/schools/magickey

History
http://www.ancientegypt.co.uk/menu.html

Science
http://www.nhm.ac.uk/kids-only

Geography at KS1
http://www.bbc.co.uk/schools/barnabybear/

RE for Early Years
http://www.dottieandbuzz.co.uk/

RE, Art, History, Culture
http://www.bl.uk/learning/cult/sacredbooks/sacredintro.html

NALDIC
http://www.naldic.org.uk/ITTSEAL2/ite/school.cfm

Song Lyrics
http://www.kididdles.com/lyrics/r035.html
http://www.sibelius.com/products/scorch/index.html

Kung Fu sentences – KS1 Bitesize activities
http://www.bbc.co.uk/schools/ks1bitesize/literacy

Teachers media - general information about supporting EAL pupils
http://www.teachersmedia.co.uk/videos/ks1-ks2-english-the-multilingual-school
http://www.teachersmedia.co.uk/videos/kung-fu-physics
http://www.teachersmedia.co.uk/videos/ks1-ks2-english-the-multilingual-school
http://www.teachersmedia.co.uk/videos/managing-eal-primary-assessing-
speaking
http://www.teachersmedia.co.uk/videos/managing-eal-primary-assessing-writing
http://www.teachersmedia.co.uk/videos/english-as-an-additional-language
http://www.teachersmedia.co.uk/videos/eal-1
http://www.teachersmedia.co.uk/videos/eal-lost-in-translation-part-1
http://www.teachersmedia.co.uk/videos/eal-lost-in-translation-part-2
http://www.teachersmedia.co.uk/videos/ks1-ks2-eal-talking-eal-at-green-end-
primary

Teachernet.gov
http://www.teachernet.gov.uk/teachingandlearning/library/EALteaching/

The Singing Playground
http://www.vam.ac.uk/vastatic/microsites/1513_singing_playground/index.html
http://www.singup.org/songbank/song-bank/song-detail/view/107-singing-
playgrounds
http://www.singup.org/magazine/magazine-article/view/27-start-your-own-
singing-playground

Appendices

Appendices

Appendix 1

Musical scores and lyrics

Heads, Shoulders, Knees and Toes

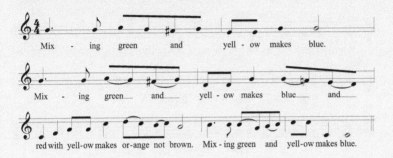

Heads, shoulders, knees and toes, knees and toes (sing and touch each body part)
Heads, shoulders, knees and toes, knees and toes (sing and touch each body part)
Eyes and ears and mouth and nose (sing and touch each body part)
Heads, shoulders, knees and toes, knees and toes (sing and touch each body part)

Repeat the verse but don't repeat the first word - hum it instead so that
eventually you end up humming the whole of the verse, i.e.

Hum, shoulders, knees and toes, knees and toes (sing and touch each body
part)
Hum, shoulders, knees and toes, knees and toes (sing and touch each body part)
Eyes and ears and mouth and nose (sing and touch each body part)
Hum, shoulders, knees and toes, knees and toes (sing and touch each body part)

Hum, *Hum-hum*, knees and toes, knees and toes (sing and touch each body part)
Hum, *Hum-hum*, knees and toes, knees and toes (sing and touch each body part)
Eyes and ears and mouth and nose (sing and touch each body part)
Hum, *Hum-hum*, knees and toes, knees and toes (sing and touch each body part)

etc.

Sing to Remember

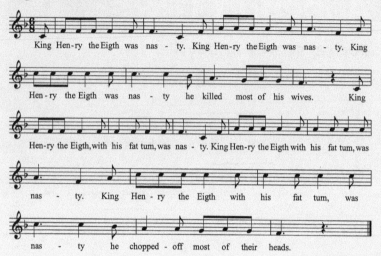

King Hen-ry the Eigth was nas - ty. King Hen-ry the Eigth was nas - ty. King Hen-ry the Eigth was nas - ty he killed most of his wives. King Hen-ry the Eigth, with his fat tum, was nas - ty. King Hen-ry the Eigth with his fat tum, was nas - ty. King Hen - ry the Eigth with his fat tum, was nas - ty he chopped - off most of their heads.

Using the same tune as *'One Finger, One Thumb, Keep Moving'* you can create lyrics such as:

King Henry the VIII was nasty (x 3)
He killed most of his wives!

King Henry the VIII with his fat tum was nasty (x 3)
He chopped off most of their heads!

King Henry the VIII with his fat tum who spent lots of money was nasty (x 3)

But some wives did survive!

Oranges and Lemons

Name: _____

Date: _____

Or - ang - es and lem - ons say the bells of St. Clemm- ents. I

owe you five farth - ings say the bells of St. Mar - tins.

When will you pay me say the bells of Old Bai- ley. When I grow rich, say the bells of Shore

ditch. When will that be, say the bells of Step- ney. I'm sure I don't know says the

great bell of Bow. Here comes a can-dle to light you to bed. Here comes the

chopp-er to chop off your head. Chip, chop, chip

chop. The last man's head comes right Off!

Oranges and lemons
Say the bells of St Clements
I owe you five farthings
Say the bells of St Martins
When will you pay me?
Say the bells of Old Bailey
When I grow rich
Say the bells of Shoreditch
When will that be?
Say the bells of Stepney
I'm sure I don't know
Says the great bell of Bow

Here comes a candle to light you to bed
Here comes the chopper to chop off your head!

Chip, Chop, Chip, Chop

The last man's head comes right off!

(arms come down!)

Ring a Ring of Roses

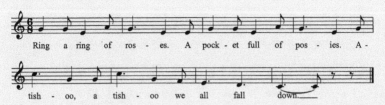

Ring, a ring of roses,
A pocket full of posies;
Atishoo, atishoo,
All stand still. (*Keep moving clockwise*)

The King has sent his daughter,
To fetch a pail of water;
Atishoo, atishoo,
We all fall down! (*Fall down and crouch on the floor*)

The bird upon the steeple, (*whisper*)
Sits high above the people; (*whisper*)
Atishoo, atishoo,
All kneel down. (*Children kneel down on the floor*)

The wedding bells are ringing, (*loudly*)
The boys and girls are singing; (*loudly*)
Atishoo, atishoo,
All fall down. (*Children fall to the floor sneezing*)

The cows are in the meadow
Eating buttercups.
Atishoo, atishoo,
We all jump up! (*Children jump up*)

This rhyme is repeated.

Teddy Bear

Teddy bear Teddy bear
Turn around
Teddy bear Teddy bear
Touch the ground
Teddy bear Teddy bear
Touch your shoe
Teddy bear Teddy bear
That will do!
Teddy bear Teddy bear
Switch off the light
Teddy bear Teddy bear
Say good night!

Miss Susie had a Baby!

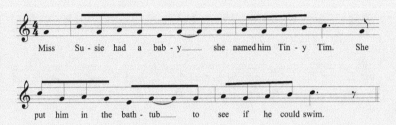

Miss   Su - sie   had   a   bab - y____   she   named him   Tin - y   Tim.   She

put   him   in   the   bath - tub____   to   see   if   he   could swim.

Miss Susie had a baby,
She named him Tiny Tim
She put him in the bathtub,
To see if he could swim.

He drank up all the water
He ate up all the soap,
He tried to eat the bathtub
But it wouldn't go down his throat.

Miss Susie called the doctor,
Miss Susie called the nurse,
Miss Susie called the lady,
With the alligator purse.

In came the doctor,
In came the nurse,
In came the lady,
With the alligator purse.

Mumps said the doctor,
Measles said the nurse,
Hiccups said the lady
With the alligator purse

Miss Susie punched the doctor,
Miss Susie kicked the nurse,
Miss Susie thanked the lady
With the alligator purse.

The Farmer's in the Dell

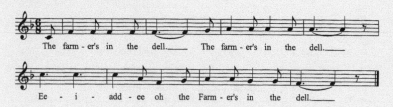

The farmer's in the dell
The farmer's in the dell
Ee-i-add-ee oh
The farmer's in the dell

The Telephone Song

Hey Us-man   I think I hear my   name. Hey Us-,man,   I think I hear it a- gain. You're

wan-ted on the   tel-e phone.___Well if it's not Is-a-bell-a then I'm not at___ home. With a

rick-tick rick-ety tick____ oh, yeah. With a rick-tick tick-et-y tick.__

Group: *Hey Usman*
X: *I think I hear my name!*
Group: *Hey Usman*
X: *I think I hear it again!*
Group: *You're wanted on the telephone!*
X: *Well if it's not Isabella then I'm not at home!*
Group: *with a rick-tick rick-ety tick*

This is repeated until all the children have been chosen to sing or it's playtime.

Queenie I

Group: *Queenie I, Queenie I who's got the ball?*

Leader chooses a child by saying their name and asking if they have it

Child 1: *I haven't got it, it isn't in my pocket!*
Group: *Queenie I Queenie I who's got the ball?*

Child chooses a different child

Child 2: *I haven't got it, it isn't in my pocket*
Group: *Queenie I Queenie I who's got the ball?*

This is repeated three times. If the leader hasn't realised who has the ball then the child who had it becomes the next leader and a new set of children are chosen.

This is the way we . . .

This is the way that we stay safe
We stay safe
We stay safe
This is the way that we stay safe
For a school fire alarm

Appendix 2

Writing frames

An example of a writing frame for a written account of a topic:

> Although I already knew that . . .
> I have learnt some new facts. I learnt that . . .
> I also learnt that . . .
> However the most interesting thing I learnt was . . .

An example of a writing frame for persuasive writing:

> Although not everybody would agree, I want to argue that . . .
> I have several reasons for arguing this point of view.
> My first reason is . . .
> Another reason is . . . because . . .
> Furthermore . . .
> Therefore . . .
> In conclusion . . .

The Minibeast classification game

The game overleaf helps children to categorise and sort minibeasts. It requires children to know about the characteristics of minibeasts and encourages discussion. It is best to put the children in mixed-ability groups of two or three.

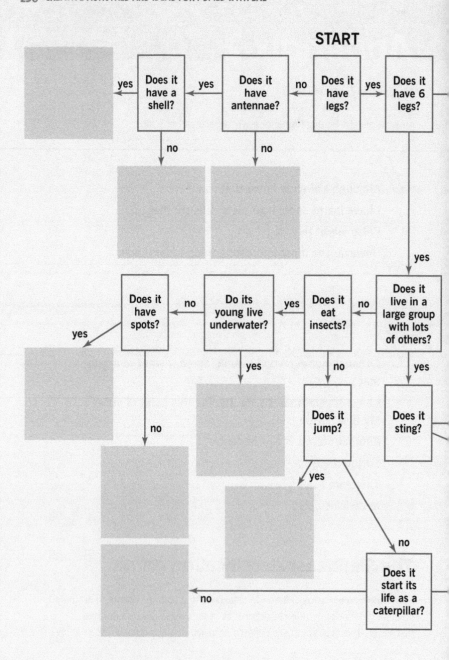

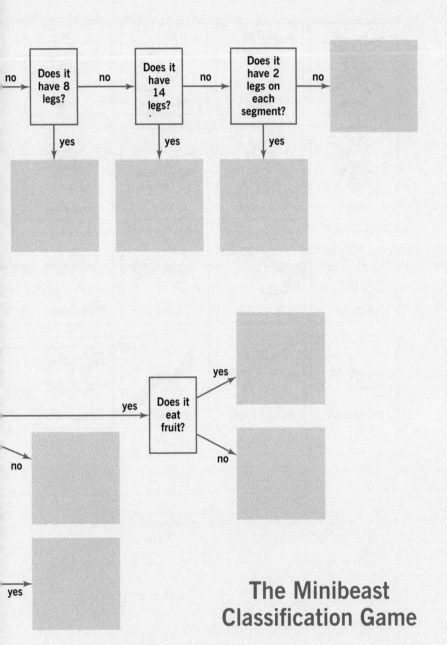

no → Does it have 8 legs? → no → Does it have 14 legs?. → no → Does it have 2 legs on each segment? → no

yes ↓ (from "Does it have 8 legs?")

yes ↓ (from "Does it have 14 legs?")

yes ↓ (from "Does it have 2 legs on each segment?")

yes → Does it eat fruit? → yes

no

no

yes

The Minibeast Classification Game